Cooperating Congregations

Portraits of Mission Strategies

Gilson A.C. Waldkoenig and William O. Avery

Foreword by James W. Lewis

An Alban Institute Publication

Scripture quotations, unless otherwise noted, are from the New Revised Standard Version of the Bible, copyright © 1989, Division of Christian Education of the National Council of the Churches of Christ in the United States of America, and are used by permission.

Library of Congress Card Number 99-69574
ISBN 1-56699-225-7

For

Kathleen D. Avery,

Spanish teacher

Mi amiga, mi esposa

—William O. Avery

For

Kirstin and Jonah,

who love good stories

—Gilson Waldkoenig

CONTENTS

Acknowledgments   vii

Foreword   ix

Introduction   1

Chapter 1. Tri-County Ministry, North Dakota   15

Chapter 2. North Central Cluster, West Virginia   49

Chapter 3. Upper Sand Mountain Parish, Alabama   79

Chapter 4.   Milwaukee Strategy, Wisconsin   111

Chapter 5. Mission at the Eastward, Maine   147

Chapter 6. Conclusion: Key Features of Cooperative Ministry   187

Appendix   Guidance for Beginning a Cooperative   203

Notes   205

ACKNOWLEDGMENTS

Many people contributed time and support for this book to be written. We want to thank all those who graciously allowed us to interview them at the five locations. Many accommodated our schedules by giving up time on the weekend. Especially, we offer our heartfelt gratitude to the leaders of these cooperatives, who arranged the interviews and were hosts to us during our visits—the Rev. Kelly Marshall, the Rev. Dorsey Walker, the Rev. Carell Foss, the Rev. Richard Deines, and the Rev. Scott Planting. These directors also read the chapters on their respective clusters and, while they may not have agreed with everything we wrote, helped us get the factual information correct.

We hired local researchers for each site to provide important background on the cooperatives and the areas where the coalitions are located. Michael Greenhour was our researcher for North Central Cluster, Tammy Werner for Tri-County, the Rev. Michael Bonham for USMP, Delmar Voter for MATE, and the Rev. Richard Deines for Milwaukee. Matthew Lenahan transcribed many audiotapes of the interviews. Katie Deighan, administrative assistant for field education, Mary Beth Schramm, assistant for field education, and Kari Olsen, secretary for faculty, dealt with the many versions of the manuscript—duplicating, sending copies to various people, and supporting the authors in their work in many ways. We thank them all.

We thank the many students at the Lutheran Theological Seminary in Gettysburg, Pennsylvania, who have stimulated our thinking, questioned our assumptions, and helped us clarify our conclusions. We especially thank the class in "The Story of Faith and Money in American

Protestantism" (spring semester, 1999). The students gave helpful feedback to the first draft of this material and, in the process, became enthusiastic about cooperative ministry.

We also thank the staff of Alban Institute. James P. Wind, president of Alban, encouraged us to pursue our initial ideas about this project and research design. Our editors, especially David Lott and Jean Caffey Lyles, gave detailed suggestions and offered that indispensable function that editors perform for authors. L. Shannon Jung, of the Center for Theology and Land, and the Rev. Louise Knotts, of the Town and Country Church Institute, read the manuscript and gave much-appreciated comments.

We could not have done the research for this book without a generous research grant from the Louisville Institute. We want to thank the institute and its director, James Lewis, for recognizing the importance of the topic and offering crucial suggestions that helped to shape our research. We especially thank him for writing the foreword to this book.

Finally, we want to thank two people who faithfully supported us and offered editorial suggestions—our spouses, Kathleen D. Avery and Amy F. Waldkoenig.

WILLIAM O. AVERY
GILSON A. C. WALDKOENIG

FOREWORD

This short book undertakes three large tasks. At one level, *Cooperating Congregations* describes a distinctive and little-known organizational structure—the cooperative parish. Second, it tells striking stories of creative congregational adaptation. Third, in light of both structure and stories, it evokes a lively hope that even hard-pressed outposts of Christian life in the United States can both survive and live faithfully in these times.

Though a hopeful book, it is also a painfully realistic one. As the authors acknowledge early and often, most congregations in the United States are small, and many are getting smaller by the year, even as the costs of maintaining a full-time parish program continue to rise. As a result, the "one pastor for one church" model is almost a thing of the past in many rural and inner-city locations. But, as the five cooperative parishes described here can testify, there are more ways of "doing church" than the freestanding congregation served by a sole pastor.

Perhaps one of the most creative options for small congregations is the model proposed in these pages—the cooperative parish. In reality, as you will see, the cooperative parish is not so much a single institutional model as a variety of ways of combining extensive institutional cooperation with congregational autonomy. The authors focus on five separate cooperative parishes, ranging in age from nine to forty-six years old. Although their organizational structures are varied, they share several common features. In all of them, vision and leadership are crucial to the success of the parish. Moreover, this visionary leadership is exercised by both clergy and lay leaders. Indeed, the cooperative parish seems to be especially fertile ground for the development of lay leaders.

There is, however, no romanticism here. Not all of these cooperative parishes work equally well, and some tensions appear to be almost inevitable.

Although Waldkoenig and Avery point to solid achievements in all five of them, including the survival of their constituent congregations, cooperative parishes are not principally about congregational survival. To the contrary, as the authors insist repeatedly, successful cooperative parishes are driven more by a passion for Christian mission than by a struggle for survival.

It is this passion for mission that fuels their creativity and enables them to adapt in imaginative ways to settings that are basically hostile to traditional congregational life: broad stretches of prairie country that are losing both their economic base and their young people; a poverty-stricken southern Appalachian plateau; a far-flung mountain region in West Virginia; an area of poverty in a segregated rust belt city; and a swath of impoverished rural New England. Congregations in such demanding settings, the authors tell us, are most likely to thrive when they move beyond a concern for survival and toward a commitment to mission. Even as they face daunting institutional challenges to their very existence, they are often able to live faithfully when they look beyond their walls to minister to the suffering communities in which they are located. One effective way of doing so, in at least some settings, is the cooperative parish.

Waldkoenig and Avery do not claim too much for the cooperative parish. It is certainly no panacea for small congregations. But they seek to convince the reader that the cooperative parish model is one creative, adaptive, and relatively unknown resource which ought to be in the toolbox of small church pastors and denominational officials. They persuaded me.

Although recent literature in congregational studies has drawn attention to a wide variety of congregations, the story of the contemporary cooperative parish is not well known. In her *Congregation and Community* (New Brunswick: Rutgers University Press, 1997), recounting her study of numerous congregations around the United States, Nancy Ammerman emphasizes the remarkable ability of congregations to adapt to changing circumstances. Although no cooperative parish appears in her study, the ones studied herein confirm her conclusion. Cooperative parishes, too, have been wonderfully creative in adapting to the often difficult circumstances in which they find themselves.

In getting to know them and then introducing them to us, Gilson Waldkoenig and William Avery have given all those who care about American congregations a great gift. They remind us that cooperative parishes can be remarkably creative in discovering how to be the church in mission, adapting in the process to the challenging circumstances around them. Their story, then, is partly an account of institutional ingenuity. But, in the end, *Cooperating Congregations* is mainly a story of adaptation and of hope.

JAMES W. LEWIS
Executive Director
The Louisville Institute
Louisville, Kentucky

"It seems like the whole pattern is changing," mused a 77-year-old woman who had a long tenure of lay leadership in a small West Virginia congregation. "Whoever thought, 20 years ago, that the congregations would do as much as the pastors?" For a decade, her church had been part of a cooperative parish, coalition, or cluster. An increasingly recognized pattern, cooperatives have been particularly appealing to small and financially pressed congregations, and to the judicatories (dioceses, synods, etc.) and professional leaders who hold responsibility for them. Today many people are beginning to see that cooperative parishes foster appropriate transformation and inspire adaptive responses to contextual change.

Congregational Crisis

American congregations have been hard-pressed in recent years by financial problems, declining membership, and the troubles of attracting and holding clergy. A few congregations have grown to become megachurches, and there have been a myriad of new church starts. However, small congregations make up the majority of Protestant churches in the United States and Canada. Half of U.S. Protestant congregations have an average weekly worship attendance of fewer than 75, and approximately three-fifths have fewer than 100.[1] In this study we will examine cooperatives in the Methodist, Episcopal, Lutheran, and Presbyterian traditions. All of these denominations have been losing members since the 1960s. Small congregations and declining membership mean not only reduced financial resources but also financial crises. An observer of the Episcopal Church could be writing for all the traditional mainline churches: "It is no longer possible to assume that a significant majority of congregations have the resources to employ a full-time seminary trained priest as well as [to] support building facilities, program, and outside giving."[2] The increasing age of members is another factor in mainline denominations. In the Evangelical Lutheran Church in America (ELCA), for example, the average age is 54, while the average age in the general U.S. population is 32.[3] Given this information on age and decline, some experts predict that by the year 2025, two-thirds of the Protestant churches in this country will be unable to support their own pastor.

Reasons for congregations to consider cooperative arrangements include: small memberships, declining attendance, and financial difficulties.[4] The sheer number of congregations that are or will be unable to afford a pastor on their own is reason enough to consider alternative staffing arrangements. Cooperatives provide a lively option.

The Cooperative Model

Cooperative parishes are clusters of congregations that have joined together to engage in common mission and to share resources, without surrendering individual congregational identity or consolidating in the usual sense of the term. Cooperatives have greater structural integrity than the traditional circuit or yoked parish, in which only the preacher (and perhaps a parsonage) is shared between (or among) autonomous congregations. On the other hand, most cooperatives declare in their foundational documents that their intention is not to merge or to close individual congregations. The vision is to enhance and extend the ministries of the congregations within a concerted area mission for the sake of the whole church.

The cooperative parish offers possibilities for vibrant witness and community outreach for many congregations. However, the model is not a one-size-fits-all answer for the troubles of small congregations, nor is it a panacea for the plight of the church's mission in our time. At one time, rural- and small-church advocates argued that cooperatives would turn these congregations into efficient modernized institutions. Many also believed that consolidation would necessarily follow cooperative arrangements, just as schools, shopping, and health care consolidated throughout the 20th century. Such merging of congregations has happened only in selective situations, and the small church remains decentralized all across the American landscape. Today the pendulum has swung back toward an emphasis on decentralization.

Thus, some small-church consultants view arrangements such as clustering, which preserves the integrity of the local church, as a strategic positioning for future mission.

Alternatives

Other strategies besides the cooperative parish can promote congregational interaction. The labeling of types, which varies from one denomination to another, can become confusing. The authors of this book recognize the variety of nomenclature in American church life and respect the integrity of ecclesiological traditions that inform the use of certain terms. A brief typology for descriptive purposes will help to delineate the specific subjects studied in this book.

1. Circuit or Yoke

A circuit or yoked parish has a lone pastor shared between or among congregations, with little or no other programmatic interaction. The circuit is the traditional colonial and frontier method of mission in American religious history. The congregations of a circuit or yoke are completely autonomous except for sharing a pastor. If there is a central council for a yoked parish, it does little more than provide for pastoral compensation. Increased centralized programming and finances move a yoked parish toward the cooperative model.

2. Satellites

Satellite or extended ministries are situations in which a stronger church helps a weaker or newer one. The stronger church is not affected in institutional structure, authority, or governance. A different kind of congregational cooperation involves the sharing of facilities. The historic "union churches" of German Reformed and Lutheran congregations in the eastern Pennsylvania countryside are one example. The congregations maintained separate liturgies, membership rolls, councils, ministers, and denominational affiliations, but they met in a jointly owned building and often shared a common Sunday school. In some contemporary situations mission congregations for recent immigrant populations share space for a time in an established congregation's building.

3. Consolidation

Consolidations and mergers take place when congregations organically combine as institutions. Sometimes this unification means moving to a new physical site together and assuming a new congregational name. At other times one congregation absorbs another. The terminology of consolidations and mergers varies from denomination to denomination, but the defining point is that one congregation or both lose institutional independence in favor of a new arrangement.

Advantages of Cooperatives

Cooperative or cluster parishes differ from the alternatives cited above in a number of ways. A central council coordinates program or mission in a cooperative parish. There is a centrally called staff—be it a single resource person or director, or an entire pastoral staff compensated by the central council on behalf of the entire cooperative. Some degree of budget consolidation exists, although the budget may not be totally centralized. The cooperative budget might be merely a common fund made up of congregational subscriptions—not very different from the systems in many yoked parishes. The clear intention in a cooperative, however, is to plan united mission among the congregations under common staff leadership. Cooperative parishes may be composed of congregations equal in size, or one congregation may be larger than the others and serve as a "cathedral" or anchor to the parish. The latter case has affinities to the satellite model above, but differs in that the cathedral church becomes a full partner in the cooperative, not merely an outside contributor. Cooperative parishes may be denominationally homogenous or ecumenical.

The flexible nature of cooperatives leads to a number of advantages:

1. Renewal of Mission

The cooperative parish can renew congregations in mission. By forming a cooperative, congregations consistently change from being turned in upon themselves to adapting a mission stance of service beyond the walls of their churches. Preoccupation with survival is widespread in small-membership congregations. But cooperatives have led many small congregations into a mission posture, serving the local community and the wider public. At the same time, their immediate future and the promise of weekly services with a pastor are assured. The cooperative arrangement creates a new entity more adept at defining area mission needs and helping congregations work together at addressing those needs. In turn, through their joint mission, these congregations begin to think of the church in a collective sense. Larger churches, too, may find in the cooperative strategy a renewed approach to local outreach.

2. Lay Ministry

Lay leadership develops in the cooperative model. The comments of the 77-year-old woman, with which we began this chapter, are an example of a dramatic shift in vision and mission that cooperative parishes embody. All baptized members are missionaries of the church; congregations are out-posts for worldwide mission, not self-contained institutions; pastors are missioners, not professionalized experts; and judicatories are secondary resource providers to the frontline work of congregations—not authorities calling the shots. These indicators have been imagined and yearned for by many visionary people in the church. To many, these indicators epitomize a faithful church in our time. But for others, the movement from the paradigm of "one pastor, one congregation," is a sign of painful accommodation to institutional and spiritual decline in the Christian church.[5]

3. Community Ministry

Cooperative parishes have a proven record of wide and effective local community impact. Through a cooperative, congregations can do more than they would be able to do on their own, and they can set up extra-congregational structures that are often necessary for community-building projects.

Christians speak with a more unified voice when they address local community issues as a cooperative. While cooperation has some effect on internal congregational issues, such as ensuring pastoral services to members, cooperative parishes really show their strengths in community outreach. Through cooperatives, the church can help to sustain local communities.

4. Adaptability in the American Environment

Defined by its mission, the church is free to express itself institutionally in a variety of ways. Cooperative parishes are institutional expressions of the church that enhance the church's viability in the modern American social environment. Cooperatives are striking cases of the institutional malleability of American congregational life. They maintain the historic catholic sense of parish while taking advantage of the American voluntaristic environment. American religion has succeeded partly because of the prominent role of individual initiative and choice.

One reason that American Christians are very active is that they can choose their churches and influence their makeup. On the other hand, a sense of community has not been sustained on the basis of choice alone but has depended upon a sense of belonging based on local identity. Often ethnicity has reinforced local identity, further compensating in the communal aspect of religion against the prevalence of individual choice. Increasingly in the postmodern world, local identity is severely challenged and ethnic enclaves eroded.

Cooperatives provide a balance between community and individual choice, and can hold these two in fruitful tension. On one hand, cooperatives help congregations to avoid becoming communal islands. When the church becomes simply a part of localized community, it cannot hear dissenting views or prophetic messages. On the other hand, cooperatives help congregations to avoid becoming merely associations of like-minded individuals. When the church is simply a matter of individual choice, then one opinion seems as valid as any other. Cooperatives can hold these two forces in tension, accomplishing a balance that has been difficult to maintain in the American social environment.

5. Organic Development

Furthermore, cooperatives foster the organic development of congregations. Congregations today must embrace change. Change is happening
constantly, and congregations need strong leadership and a great deal of
nurture to grow in, with, and through change. Congregations, like all human
communities, have distinctive capabilities and limitations in how much and
how rapidly they can change. Healthy growth and sustainable community
arise organically from who and what people are, paced in stages appropriate to the capacities to change of those involved.

Cooperating congregations allow for adaptive change for individual
congregations. They are penultimate responses to social change, allowing
for a variety of outcomes. If congregations must merge or consolidate, they
may grow together first through cooperative arrangements. If one must
close, it may do so with dignity because of the sustained presence of the
church's continuing local ministry through the cooperative. If congregations
must part to go in different mission directions, cooperative structures are
easily retired. If handled well, a cooperative arrangement can be a setting
for rebuilding, out of which congregations can rise to take advantage of
new opportunities.

6. A Rich Alternative

The cooperative parish is a lively alternative to other popular but ultimately
unproductive strategies for providing pastoral services to small congregations. In well-populated areas, it is easy for judicatories and congregations
to recycle retired pastors in small congregations. Such arrangements often
favor the status quo and deny small congregations the fresh energy of new
leadership. On the other hand, many small congregations are treated as
stepping-stones for pastors fresh from seminary. Congregational members
then experience rapid pastoral turnover, and the lack of stability in pastoral
leadership thwarts community outreach.

Cooperative parishes provide feasible, challenging calls for ordained
ministers in the prime of their careers. Meanwhile, certified lay ministries,
diaconal ministries, and other officially recognized forms of service have an
opportunity to become established and thrive alongside ordained ministry
within cooperative parishes. Independent small congregations that do little

more than employ a retired or inexperienced pastor for services, funerals, and weddings can only dream of additional life-enhancing ministries such as parish nursing, professional counseling, and community services. The cooperating congregations can enrich church and community life by providing the same standard of diverse and well-trained leadership that other segments of the church enjoy today.

Responses "for the Meantime"

The perspective we have carried throughout our research and writing is that cooperatives are "for the meantime" responses of the ecumenical church to a trying period for institutions in American society. Cooperatives *might* turn out to be efficient steps toward consolidation, or they *might* be the gestation of new decentralized mission for the 21st century. In this book, we present snapshots of the experiences of Christians in different contexts, portraits of how Christians are experimenting with a broader functional definition of the local church than the typical American sense of "congregation." The congregations in this book have all ventured beyond the institutional patterns that most Americans recall. In place of individualistic competition between local churches, the practice of cooperatives suggests the ancient Christian idea of the parish as a place; i.e., an area ministry to whole communities and not only to congregational members. Along with such internal transformation comes a renewed bond between church and community, as the clustering congregations share the cooperative spirit with other institutions of their localities.

What happens when congregations are not independent, entrepreneurial organizations competing with one another for their own survival, in a marketing game to attract the most members? The emerging cooperative pattern of church life defies what sociologist Stephen Warner calls "the de-facto congregationalism" of American life.[6] Cooperative parishes may be the beginning of widespread congregational restructuring for a new age of mission in the North American church, or they may be merely a symptom of a time of institutional decline and financial stress. Be that as it may, cooperatives in the time of this study were interesting institutional configurations that certain visionary and energetic church people built from the grass roots in some particular places. Cooperatives have harbored living expressions of everyday, local communal life in the late 20th century.

They are in themselves worthy of study because they are distinctive phenomena in American society and religion.

Cooperatives are also worthy of study for theological reasons. If there is a pervasive bias on the part of the authors, it is that God works creatively through Christian congregations. This bias has been reinforced by our glimpses of the oft-overlooked but profound beauty of local people's hopes and dreams for authentic Christian mission in their time and place. In our research, we heard and sensed a transformational reality that has always been foundational for the Christian experience. Each of us carried definitions of the church and its work in the world into this study. Because such frames of reference influence the study process, we offer now a brief word of description on those theological and ecclesiological commitments.

One of us emphasizes that the mission of the church and every congregation is to be a foretaste of the Kingdom of God. The church's mission is (1) to engage people in the coming Kingdom, through its witness and worship, and (2) to work for shalom (justice, wholeness, peace, and harmony) in the world. Like Jesus, the church is a suffering servant that takes up its cross in solidarity with those who are suffering, seeking justice for the oppressed. The church in mission and service points beyond itself, participating in the Kingdom of God *proleptically*.

"By *prolepsis*," says theologian Ted Peters, "I mean anticipation of future reality in a concrete preactualization of it." With Peters, one holds that "Jesus Christ is the future made present. He is the first-fruits (1 Cor. 15:20)."[7] Hence one looks for the church of Jesus Christ to show signs of participating in that same reality.

The other author emphasizes that congregations are means of grace insofar as they are the crucibles out of which springs the living Word for the sake of the world. This study shows, from the empirical evidence of five cooperatives, a reliable vision of the active work of God through the church in the world. Such work may or may not be in formal continuity with the coming Kingdom described above; i.e., it may be more penultimate than ultimate in form. Nevertheless, "hidden deep in the flesh" of Christian congregational experience, and therefore the cooperative parish experience, is the living presence of Christ.

The Research

We traveled to the parishes profiled in this book between August 1997 and December 1998. At each site we conducted numerous structured interviews with staff and lay members. Usually, we made two visits of four to five days in duration. We made one trip to Milwaukee. Our design was to gather the stories, worries, dreams, and hopes of the very people who have been experimenting with cooperative or cluster structures.

We were aware of denominationally produced literature and a few other publications that present the cooperative concept.[8] This literature consists primarily of "how to" guides and promotional pieces. We recommend the best of these in the appendix. What was lacking was any study of the actual experiences of people in cooperative congregations. Inspired by recent books and methodologies that employ the voices of church people and their narratives in context, we set out with a template of questions to learn and compare the stories of five cooperative parishes in four denominations and in five areas of the United States.[9]

We chose denominationally affiliated clusters because we assumed that more possibility of cross-congregational institutional development would arise between denominational partners than in multidenominational cooperatives. That assumption should be checked by a parallel study of interdenominational cooperatives—a project that we hope someone will complete in the future.

Our choice of sites arose in the following way. Through publications on rural and small-church ministries, we were aware of the longevity and excellent reputations of two cooperatives—Mission at the Eastward (Maine) and the Upper Sand Mountain Parish (Alabama). Similarly, through an outreach video of the Evangelical Lutheran Church in America, we learned about Tri-County Ministry in North Dakota.[10] Through a book by an Episcopal bishop, we learned of the North Central Cluster of West Virginia.[11] Through the ELCA's urban coalition network we knew also of the cooperative in Milwaukee. Conversations with key officials in each denomination confirmed and directed us to our choices.

The quotations we report were responses to a template of questions that covered four topical areas: lay experience, clergy experience, lay and clergy interaction, and visions of the church. In methodology we were committed to an oral historical procedure in which we granted the integrity and importance of the narrative arising in each interview. Hence, our template of questions, while consistent throughout the project, bore fruit in different ways, depending on the conditions and experiences of each study site. We hope that our book will inspire additional studies using other methodologies that probe in ways not possible in our approach. At the same time, we believe that our bias toward narrative integrity, the "storied" approach that our methods assiduously upheld, will be helpful to a variety of other researchers and practitioners.[12]

Structure of Each Chapter

For the sake of readers, the case studies are organized in this book in parallel ways, so that comparison and contrast of the cooperatives is readily accessible:

1. *Introduction and context.* Each chapter begins with a snapshot of life in the cooperative. A description of the context follows. Here we are attentive to the distinctive geography, economy, and local culture in which the cooperative parish functions.

2. *Development.* The story of the cooperative's development in that context follows, with attention to the hopes and dreams, as well as the aches and pains, of the founding generation.

3. *Ministries.* A section on the ministries and projects of the parish gives readers a sense of the continuing work of the cooperative. Here the accomplishments that are possible only through collective action receive most attention.

4. *Vision.* The visions of leaders and people are the subjects of the next two sections in each chapter. How people understand mission and ministry, and how they view the church local and universal, are features of these sections. The vision of leaders broaches theological and professional issues that bear upon the public offices of ministry.

5. *Tensions.* Each chapter explores the tensions that stress and challenge the cooperatives. The tensions can be creative, destructive, and at times both. Ranging from procedural issues to the complexities of human

relationships, the sections on tensions chronicle the organizational and human landscape of cooperatives.

6.   *Why it works.* Each chapter has a section reporting the main reasons that the ministries and visions of each cooperative have been sustained over time.

7.   *Future.* Finally, the threats and promises of the future for the cooperative close each chapter. Often perceived threats were extensions of the tensions, and hopes were extensions of the factors that allow the venture to work. The social and economic context looms in determining the future as well. But new vision, fresh hopes, and some fears emerge in the final section of each chapter.

The Sites and the Structure of the Book

The first chapter describes a young but successful cooperative parish called *Tri-County Ministry*. Composed of seven congregations of the Evangelical Lutheran Church in America, and one partner from the Presbyterian Church (U.S.A), Tri-County Ministry is located in and around Cooperstown, North Dakota. Lay leaders began the cooperative in 1992, during concurrent pastoral vacancies in all the congregations. With one large and several small congregations, Tri-County sustains a staff of a lead pastor, two ordained associate pastors, one lay pastor, a seminary intern, a parish coordinator, and two support-staff members. The pastors on staff are called to the cooperative, not to individual congregations. The parish has a combined membership of about 1,300; it rotates leadership of worship services and pastoral duties among the staff.

Readers will get a sense of the experience of starting a cooperative parish from the Tri-County chapter. Laity took the lead in forming Tri-County, and a remarkable shift in attitude resulted. The local politics of restructuring the governance of the churches was a fresh memory for some, and that is profiled in the chapter. Tri-County is marked by its institutional integrity, in that the eight congregations have equal representation and call the staff in common. Those features and Tri-County's relative newness at the time of this study make it the best account to read first.

The North Central Cluster of the Episcopal Diocese of West Virginia is the second case study. Located in the center of West Virginia, in the towns of Elkins, Buckhannon, Grafton, and Bridgeport, the cluster included four small congregations at the time of this study. Although the congregations had experienced different arrangements of clustering since 1990, at the time of this study they had just emerged into a new pattern of stability. The churches having experienced rapid turnover of professional staff, which kept them at the beginning stages of cluster formation, the chapter on the North Central Cluster is a study in the aches and pains of beginning a cooperative parish. If Tri-County is a picture of what can happen when everything "clicks," the North Central Cluster is a reality check that reveals the depth and extent of some human and organizational issues that must be carefully addressed. The North Central Cluster includes the interesting feature of the bivocational, locally trained "Canon 9 priest," a model that will no doubt interest especially readers of episcopal and catholic ecclesial traditions.

We next present *Upper Sand Mountain Parish* of the United Methodist Church, located in and around Sylvania, Alabama. Begun in 1969, this cooperative consists of 11 small congregations on a mountain that straddles two counties in northeastern Alabama. Located in southern Appalachia, these two counties have special needs in education, jobs, care of dependent children, health care, and water quality. The parish rises to meet these needs, from directly feeding the hungry and putting roofs over people's heads, to improving the quality of life for youth on the mountain through excellent programming. A full-time director, five other clergy (not all full-time), a church-and-community worker, an intern, and support-staff members compose the leadership team. Readers will be overwhelmed with the scope and effectiveness of community-building ministry on Upper Sand Mountain.

The *Milwaukee Coalition* of the ELCA is profiled in chapter 4. Based in the inner city of Milwaukee, Wisconsin, but including interesting partnerships with suburban churches and churchwide structures, this cooperative consists of 27 ELCA parishes and two campus ministries. Formally constituted in 1988, but with roots extending as far back as 1973, this coalition has a full-time director who is also a member of synod staff (the local judicatory in the ELCA). The structure of the coalition is relatively loose and malleable in comparison to the organizations in the first three chapters. But it has a sinewy integrity that is essential to its coordinated positive impact on the stressful social conditions of the inner city, and the remarkable resilience that it fosters among congregations facing neighborhood change.

Mission at the Eastward (MATE), located near Farmington, Maine, is the subject of chapter 5. Begun the 1954, this cooperative consists of nine congregations of the Presbyterian Church (U.S.A.), and has at times included other Protestant congregations. Among the special ministries are a summer camping program, three housing ministries, rural community-action ministries, a rural-living center, and an economic-development ministry. MATE is a mature organization with a second-generation leader, and a long record of local community impact and wider church witness.

The book's final chapter lists the significant conclusions that arose from the study. Although the five sites differed from one another, with stories unique to their own experience, a pattern of common conclusions is well supported by similarities in the interviews. Among the important findings that will aid practitioners in settings other than cooperatives are insights about community ministry, lay empowerment, finances, governance, calls for clergy, and adaptive institutional responses for mission in our time.

CHAPTER 1

Tri-County Ministry,
North Dakota

Tri-County Ministry

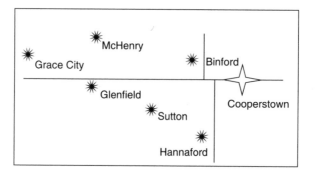

TRI-COUNTY MINISTRY

Eastern North Dakota Synod

Evangelical Lutheran Church in America

Lead pastor: The Rev. Carell Foss

Cooperative makeup: seven ELCA churches,
one Presbyterian (U.S.A.) church

Birthdate: 1992

Special Ministries: Befrienders program, gifts ministers,
confirmation mentors, parish-wide youth program

Staff: lead pastor, associate minister, associate minister
for visitation, lay pastor, a seminary intern, a parish coordinator,
and two administrative assistants

North Dakota

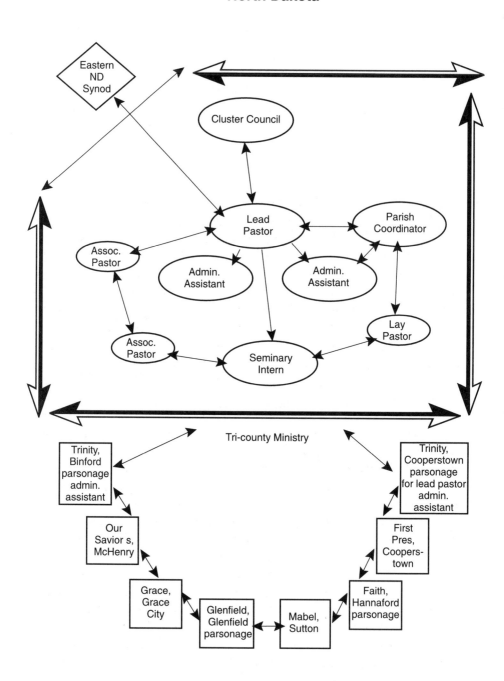

Tri-County Ministry, North Dakota

A laywoman described Tri-County Ministry as "a striped fabric. There are eight stripes, and each stripe has many strands of fibers, intertwining and strengthening each other as the strands are daily being woven into the fabric of the Tri-County Ministry." The stripes are the eight congregations, seven Lutheran and one Presbyterian, from seven towns in east-central North Dakota. "Our fabric is sturdy," the woman observed, noting that it "has the unmistakable look of a handcrafted work." It was not "perfectly even," "regular," "symmetrical," or "predictable," she acknowledged. "It's got a few lumps and bumps, and there are open ends, as is right with a work in progress," she added. Nevertheless, the woman believed that "even though it is not finished, it is already serving as our tent, and the friendship of God is upon it."

Trinity Lutheran Church of Cooperstown, North Dakota, was the anchor of the tent of friendship called Tri-County Ministry. With an average attendance of 165 per Sunday, Trinity would be capable of sustaining on its own a full-time pastor and some part-time additional staff. With vision for a stronger area ministry and the benefits of more full-time staff, however, Trinity entered cooperative negotiations with the smaller congregations of Hannaford, Binford, Sutton, Glenfield, McHenry, and Grace City. Later the small Presbyterian congregation located one block from Trinity joined the talks to complete the 40-mile-wide parish of cooperating congregations. Attendance at the smaller congregations hovered around 25 to 30 in most, with Sutton dropping to an average of 15 when the agricultural year's necessities reduced its usual high of 30. Binford, Sutton, and Hannaford are located in a north-to-south crescent in Griggs County, with 18-, 16-, and 12-mile drives from Cooperstown, respectively. Glenfield, McHenry, and Grace City form a triangle in Foster County, 21, 29, and 40 driving miles from

Cooperstown, respectively. The name Tri-County refers to Griggs and Foster counties, and neighboring Eddy County, which McHenry borders.

Entering Tri-County Ministry, the cooperating churches hoped to weave "a program of shared ministry among . . . area congregations, with a team ministry, shared staff and an area council representing each of the congregations." The hope was "to strengthen local congregations and to provide long-term stability and a quality ministry." Because they would be working together, "pastors and staff members would be there to help and advise each other, and to plan a ministry that would make use of the strengths of each member of the pastoral staff and of the people in the congregations." "Increased opportunities for youth ministry and social services" were leading goals of the venture, along with "diversity of leadership" that would assure "depth in ministry." The founders of the cooperative hoped "to create an encompassing Christian community among all the congregations involved" that would foster a "working relationship among congregations [to] provide consistency in programming" and among other benefits "provide support and challenge for pastoral staff."[1]

The vision was largely realized over the first five years of Tri-County Ministry. The cooperative exemplified organizational integrity even as it preserved the autonomy of the eight churches. Its accomplishment was no mean feat in an area hard-pressed to maintain community institutions in the face of economic and demographic decline.

Context

Flatter than the flatlands of the Great Plains are the railroad beds that span its vast reaches. Railroad builders filled crevices and boggy areas to smooth the slight undulations of the otherwise prostrate landscape. In the center of Cooperstown, North Dakota, one may stand on an empty railroad bed and gaze down the smooth ribbon where rails formerly tied the town to a booming national farm economy. The perfectly horizontal corridor without its tracks evokes an eerie sense that the enduring mark of humankind upon this landscape is a vacuous monument to migration and emigration.

North Dakota has been losing population since the 1930s. Farming has been the staple means of livelihood since settlement in the 19th century, but farm income has plummeted in the crises born of globalization and deregulation. Heaped upon the century-long "rural flight" from the Midwest is a declining birthrate throughout the region. North Dakota births declined 44 percent over the past four decades.[2] The small towns in Griggs, Foster, and Eddy counties which Tri-County Ministry serves are withering. The people are hard-pressed to maintain basic community services such as health care, education, and culture. Cooperstown maintains some small businesses besides agriculture, but for the other communities, the Rev. Carell Foss explained, "agriculture is all they have. When the farms get [fewer], that will be the end of it."

Sheer perseverance and hard work are characteristic of the people of the northern Great Plains, especially those who remain after the tracks of others have led away and the railroad ties have been taken up with them. Tragically, some people entrench themselves in rigid adherence to patterns of behavior and community life that belong to the former era before the tracks were gone. Others reapply their characteristic perseverance and hard work in new creative ventures. The parallel to their pioneering ancestors is not lost upon those who struggle to raise the quality of life in the hard-pressed days after the railroad and the once-booming farm economy have gone.

One such heir to the pioneers is a farmer from a congregation 16 miles from Cooperstown. On a bitterly cold day when from three to five inches of snow and 50-mile-per-hour winds were on their way, he stood in the church basement and said that yesterday his neighbor went bankrupt. Shaken, because this neighbor was a hard worker who had made it though the farm crisis of the 1980s, the farmer said, "You used to be able to make one or two mistakes" in farming and still recover. Now, "you couldn't make even one mistake." With farmers disappearing and population declining before their eyes, residents like this one had to carry two or three jobs, not only to cover farm and tax burdens, but also because they were the last people standing. For example, the farmer was the last licensed electrician in the Cooperstown vicinity. He'd like to quit to concentrate wholly on the razor's-edge walk of keeping the farm solvent, but he says, "If you live in the area, you've got to help along wherever you can." He will use a skill he has for his neighbors, though it increases the risk his own operation faces.

Educated at North Dakota State University and serving as a council member in a congregation of many college-educated adults, this farmer noted that "our biggest export" from rural North Dakota is "our young people that are educated. We educate them, and they leave." He said, "It's one of the signs of a decaying economy . . . that the young people of North Dakota are not coming back." He drew the lesson for rural people everywhere:

I wonder if rural America in general isn't heading in the same direction. Whether it's here, whether it's Kansas, Texas, wherever it is. If it's rural America, it seems like it's in a state of stress. The fabric of rural America is really getting stretched thin. The economics are determining what's happening to a large extent. But if the prices for our commodities were to increase suddenly, the larger farms would buy up the smaller farmers anyway and the cycle would continue. So I don't know if there is an answer for it. If somebody's got one, I'm sure that a lot of people would like to hear it.

In this situation, the communities of the area have watched services consolidate. Especially painful was the consolidation of schools. In 1960 every town in the cooperative parish had its own high school of 100 or more students, the farmer recalled. Today two high schools serve the eastern and western halves of the parish, and there are fewer than 100 students in each, he says.

Maintaining community institutions in the Tri-County area is a challenge and an arena for potential conflict. A lay leader described the situation and drew a tempered but hopeful conclusion:

Community institutions—church, school, hospital—can unite or divide us. Our schools appear to be making progress toward a peaceful cooperation and eventual merger. The health-care facilities have a history of financial problems not unique to Cooperstown alone. Recently the entire county was involved in a massive fund drive to rescue the hospital, clinic, and nursing home. It was handled very successfully by many people. The goal was $500,000 over a three-year period in cash and pledges, and so far they have reached $448,000. Some of the people who were leaders in that project have also been involved in the Tri-County Ministry effort. I also take it as a good sign that the people of Griggs County outside of Cooperstown approved the increase in their mill levy for the county library. Cooperstown did so at an earlier date. There are, of course, financial concerns, but the message to me from the hospital drive and that library vote is that people will support something they think has value.

In forming Tri-County ministry, the church has followed the general trend toward consolidation, but the quality of its behavior was very different from that of others.

A farmer described the difference by saying that in the case of the schools, industries, and retail stores, the consolidation largely "went somewhere else" and the people of his area had to follow it. In the case of the cooperative parish, Tri-County Ministry, "It's a consolidation of staff and pastors that has come to us, as opposed to each individual congregation going someplace else." Staying with the local communities, the churches asked for more participation and responsibility on the part of the laity, building on the deep sense of local ownership. Parishioners were in turn more aware of the reality of the church's situation as an institution, the farmer believed. They were, he said, less likely to "carp" about their own needs because they knew that the church's very presence as an institution was a gift.

One lay leader was amazed that the fiercely independent people of the plains could cooperate with one another. After all, another explained, "we are somewhat cautious in our assessment of situations." She noted that "we want to be sure of what we think," and added wryly, "Notice I'm not saying that we want to be sure of the facts." In light of prevailing cultural traits that would mitigate community coordination, several members attributed the birth and success of Tri-County Ministry directly to God. "I tell you," one said, "the Holy Spirit has really worked with this whole thing, this whole thing. You just wouldn't believe it all." The fact that so many people "could agree to a single solution to the problem," the longtime resident observed, "to me is really far out— especially when you consider that some of these communities, before we started, had been rivals."

School and sports rivalries were significant, but "then there are the old rivalries where Lars, back in 1910, crossed Ole someplace in one of these other towns and they had a big fight," he recalled. Such feuds "tore the communities apart and drew a line between them. These old rivalries stand for a long time." The long-lasting effects of old feuds were only beginning to melt in the present generation. "One generation prior to this," he noted, "this whole thing [the cooperative] wouldn't have worked."

More than human rivalries separate and sometimes isolate small communities and individuals from one another in the Northern Plains. Through the long months of winter, driving even the 16 miles from Sutton to Cooperstown can be a challenge. A farmer portrayed the lethal potential of North Dakota winters, and its effect upon church efforts:

> When you've got [almost] 50 miles end to end [in Tri-County Ministry], and you've got news like . . . four to six inches of snow and 50-mile-per-hour winds on the way, it starts to make the staff a little jumpy, and rightly so. They do a lot of traveling, and some of these roads aren't exactly what you'd call "interstate" either. You talk about wide open, too. You get out in some of these places and there's nobody for five or six miles. So most of them got cell phones, they got radios or some kind of device. And nearly every farmer here has a radio or a cell phone with them at all times for [the] same reasons. Winter can kill, pure and simple.

In sum, the environmental and social context was working against the possibilities for strong institutions and rich community bonds. Nevertheless, while the situation meant for one person that "we can't project that in five years we will be viable in our present form," she could also state with satisfaction that "on the other hand, the strength is, I think, flexibility." Possibilities previously impossible among the Norwegian Lutherans of North Dakota were being born.

Residents maintain hope even as they posit contrasting futures for their area. In a speculative mood, the farmer cited above imagined the exurban migrations eventually reaching rural North Dakota. In that case, the church would be prepared for mission in the reborn communities because Tri-County had kept them alive and strong. On the other hand, and in a darker assessment, if the depopulation continues and some congregations must close, there is a place for the displaced to go. The exiles from a closed congregation have friends and fellowship established with nearby congregations.

In the meantime, before the ultimate fate of the Great Plains is determined, something creative is taking root. As the Rev. Carell Foss described the situation, "It is exciting that the people in Tri-County Ministry are willing to take risks. When the Holy Spirit calls, [the Spirit] does not give us guarantees. But [the Spirit] makes a lot of promises, and will never leave us or forsake us." Therefore, he said, "I look forward to the challenge."

Development

Tri-County Ministry was born officially on May 31, 1992, with votes of overwhelming majorities in each of the congregations involved. "How do I convey to you the excitement and optimism I feel?" asked a lay leader before the vote at Trinity, Cooperstown. She continued: "In the view of the people who worked together on the plan, the Spirit is leading us toward a clearer vision of ourselves and our ministry, and our relation to each other." Instead of the malaise of decline, there would be "problems to be solved and a goal to be reached," she suggested. It was "a challenge of faith and commitment."

Enhancing the opportunity and easing the fearfulness of the unknown, the vote for the cooperative arrangement accompanied the vote to call, as "lead pastor," a talented leader with a proven record. Carell Foss was like a dream come true for churches in a rural area. Born and raised in rural North Dakota, Foss combined large-church experience from the city of Fargo with a personal style and commitments that assured instant rapport with rural people. Following his call, Pastor Foss and the Tri-County Council completed the team with two additional pastors, an associate in ministry, two secretaries and a parish coordinator. A seminary intern served year by year whenever that could be arranged. The initial team served four years, and then a clergy couple and a new parish worker joined Pastor Foss in the fifth year of Tri-County. By 1999, Foss had announced his retirement, and the challenge of transition to a new lead pastor was imminent.

The cooperative germinated in discussions during concurrent pastoral vacancies in the Lutheran congregations in 1992. A synod staff person, the Rev. Dean Larsen, "put the bug in our ear," recalled one member at Sutton. "If there was one guy responsible for planting the seed, I'd say that Dean was." Prior to that time, he said, a cooperative "was something that we hadn't really thought about seriously." While the suggestion and ideas came from the synod, the congregations determined their own fate, as one member explained:

> We were not pushed by the synod in this direction. You know, there are some people who would like to say, well, the synod is kind of pushing or being a little more authoritative than they should be. And I don't think so. Because the idea was put there, any help we needed was rendered, if possible, and outside of that we had to pretty much sink or pull. Pretty much on our own doing.

Dean Larsen "led the discussion as we talked about the value of a team pastoral ministry," another lay leader recalled. The notion of cooperation between many congregations grew gradually among the lay leaders originally charged only with filling pastoral vacancies. "By the time we left that meeting," she remembered, "we envisioned a model for two parishes with two pastors each and a loose cooperative agreement between them." The committee members returned the next time with "the feeling that we wanted no barriers, not even parish lines." Hence, a cooperative of eight congregations came together.

The newly called ministers gained a distinct advantage when they were called to the cooperative during concurrent pastoral vacancies in all the congregations. Parish coordinator Bonnie Foss, wife of the lead pastor, remarked:

> We came at a very good time, because all the churches were open and they needed a pastor. People are more receptive in a situation like that. I think it would have been very different if we had come into a situation where there were some congregations that already had pastors, and they tried to fit these pastors into this—because of their allegiance to the congregations and not feeling that they were a pastor of all eight churches. And that is vital. We came in knowing that we didn't have an allegiance to any church, but we felt we were serving all these churches.

Meanwhile, the arrival of adequate staff was a godsend for the congregations. One pastor pondered, "I don't know what these people would do if they didn't have the cooperative." He mused that the small congregations would "have to align with another congregation" or two that would be about equal in size, and the pastor serving them would be "just spread so thin."

The common plight of the small congregation bound them together in the cooperative. One of the original planners recognized "the common threads" between the congregations, large and small. "The same things were present," he recalled. "We needed preaching, we need our parsonages filled, we want a strong youth program, and we want visitation. That just stood out," he said. "Well, how do we get that?" Working together on shared needs was the answer, even between large and small churches. The same leader spoke of Trinity's needs matching the smaller congregations, only on a different scale. "We were the largest church, maybe on the verge of one-and-a-half-pastors," he observed. "But with the budget concern I knew that we would never be able to handle that locally."

For some of the congregations, the needs brought them to the edge of desperation. One planner recalled: "I believe that when we started—and this has been forgotten about—some of the smaller churches were saying, 'If we could have two more years . . . If we could have five it would be wonderful.'" After five successful years in the cooperative, "it's almost like that was forgotten about, and it's going to go on forever," he noted with a pleased chuckle. "There aren't many that remember that," he said, "except us original people. But that was some of the real concern back then."

In a weakened condition, some of the small congregations might have felt threatened. The presence of a large church in the cooperative might have invited consolidation of the smaller entities into the larger. This was not the case, but a different concern haunted the small-church people. A leader during the formation recalled:

> I think there was a feeling of—not being gobbled up—but [that] the big church was going to dictate, saying "Thanks for coming in, but now you're only going to have church one Sunday a month." But by putting the steps in place from the beginning—they're going to have their own councils, they're going to buy the ministry services [through the cooperative], if they come into financial troubles we put into the by-laws there are ways to secede from the union if you wish. Or if the finances get difficult for a month or two, "What provisions can we take so you can still stay in the group till you reexamine your situation?" The fairness, I think, all of a sudden put that in the background; it wasn't as much of an issue. And the excitement: We said, "Hey, we've got a chance here. This isn't the end of the world."

Rather than dependency of smaller upon larger, the cooperative pushed the small congregations toward responsible self-determination. At each vote in the process of building the cooperative structure, if any individual congregation did not want to go along, it was agreed that the others would continue and build it with fewer congregations. At one point, a congregation did balk. "They were holding out to get more—of what, I don't know," explained an observer. "If they thought they could get their own pastor, then fine," said one. "But," he added, "don't use the guilt on the rest of us. We had commitments." He recalled the moment of decision. The chair asked, "Are you in?" Yes, came the reply. "They knew they could not go it alone," the observer surmised.

While the cooperative moved forward, there was still plenty of defer-
ence to congregational autonomy. The fierce independence of the people
and the investment in local congregations ensured that the cooperative would
become a confederation rather than a union. This suited most of the people,
for a prevailing characteristic of North Dakota, the local communities, and
"our Norwegian Lutheranism," said one woman, "is that we are very much
populist." Practically, this meant that "there have been cases where we
didn't like what was going on," she said, "and we've sent back word through
our representatives and it has been possible to change." The capacity to
hear what is happening in the council and to "send back our approval or
disapproval" was very important to the people. Like all good populists, the
people like to "elect a representative, and a church council, but that doesn't
mean we trust them," said one member. "No," she continued, "we have to
micromanage them." If the Tri-County Council did not refer back to local
church councils, she noted, "there would be war right away!"

The confederated nature of Tri-County suited the small congregations
most of all. A small-church member observed that "the small churches
have probably benefited from this more than the large churches," because
"it has enabled some of the smaller churches to stay solvent." He questioned "whether that's going to be a long-term possibility." For the time
being, however, the churches had had "five years of peaceable cooperation," observed another. She believed that "whatever questions there were
at first have been resolved." Now there was "a structure for resolving new
problems that arise."

One of the great strengths of Tri-County is that it was constructed and
initiated by local lay leaders. Peers challenged peers with the realities of the
church's situation, and when it was finally decided to proceed in the cooperative model, the initiative and responsibility had come from among their
own, not from outside or from newly resident innovators. A key figure in
the founding looked back over the difficult task of leading through painful
changes:

> I took a lot of heat on the front end, and dodged some bullets. You
> know, you'd get cornered at a basketball game or a school music
> festival, and . . . "How come you're doing this, you can't do this,
> that's unconstitutional." Very educated people in the community
> coming up with things that didn't make sense but trying to say,
> "This isn't going to work." I think they are very strong supporters

of this now, but they never had the solutions. You could ask them, "You got a better idea?" and, no, they didn't want to deal with that.

A step-by-step, vote-by-vote process guided all parties through the construction of the cooperative. Majorities for going forward with the cooperative prevailed at every vote, according to the leader quoted above, "but the minority always talked the loudest." He recalled that dissenters had the power to "throw out the questions that we didn't have all the answers to," and to use those to stall the process temporarily. His strategy as a leader was to try to keep the group on one task at a time, saying "Um, we have to solve *this* problem," and by bringing each item "to the people" because "it was their decision."

The people chose to move forward, and "going forward, I felt guided," said a lay leader, referring to a Presence who transcends the rule of democratic process. "I gave it so much time, because we needed a well-thought-out plan. Once we got into Tri-County, we were leading 1,600-plus Lutherans with a 16-member board," and the original structure would henceforth have a crucial effect on the ministry. Thus, during the building process, the leader said, "sometimes you need to be controversial on purpose to get the interaction, just to stimulate the ideas and [ask], 'What about if we do this?'" A few years later, after the process of confrontation and deliberation was over, an enduring satisfaction remained for the leader, signified by occasions when "people that I admired—some of them deceased now— . . . would come up . . . and would say thank-you. We needed that. Thank you for doing this." He added, "As I look back, it took an awful lot of energy. It was all worth it."

Ministries

Once the lay leaders had brought Tri-County into existence, and had structured it in accordance with their own context, culture, and values, the pastoral staff could succeed in stimulating the ministry of the laity. "One of the greatest strengths of Tri-County Ministry is the lay involvement," the parish coordinator happily observed. Lay ministry was taking root throughout the parish in small groups and in structured pastoral actions by lay caregivers.

The Befrienders program engaged 19 people in consistent visitation of individuals who had had a crisis in their lives. Not meant to be counselors, the befrienders received training in basic recognition of needs so that they could make referrals to counseling professionals. The heart of befriending, however, was prayer and relationship. A by-product of this worthy ministry was stimulation of relationships across congregational lines, thus beginning to unite the parish in a common mission of prayer and love.

The Gifts Ministry equipped selected individuals to conduct worship services, to preach occasionally, and to take communion to shut-ins. A synodwide program, the Gifts Ministry allowed Tri-County an opportunity to broaden its scope of leadership. A staff member rejoiced, saying, "It's wonderful to have laypeople who are willing to do this, that don't feel that 'Hey, that's what we hired you to do, Pastor.' It's great to have laypeople who feel that they're ministers too." A vibrant sense of ministry among all the baptized is an enduring goal of the church, and church leaders in all contexts puzzle constantly over how to stimulate it. A Tri-County staff member mused: "Getting people to that point, I think, is incredible. I think that's one of our strengths" in Tri-County Ministry.

For the confirmation program, 18 mentors served as youth ministers. Meanwhile, laypeople were leading Bible studies throughout the parish. "It's really great to see the people coming out even when it's laypeople leading it," the parish coordinator said. Tri-County staff believe that "one of the keys to grow is lay involvement—getting people to feel that this is their ministry, and they can be ministers and serving someone, too."

Often laypeople have the interest and commitment for expressing their faith in acts of ministry, but the church fails to empower them with clear signs that their ministry is the church's own ministry. One gifts minister and befriender pointed out that "in some way or another what you do has to be authenticated. . . . You know, so that [those visited are] not going to think, 'Oh, there's that religious fanatic, carrying a Bible, that's coming to visit me.'" When the church publicly declares that gifts ministers and befrienders are the church's own ministers, those who receive them think, "OK, this is part of the ministry of my congregation, my church, so I will give it that respect because of the association."

Through the gifts ministers, the church goes a step further and declares that the Word of God and the sacraments are of and for the people. One gifts minister spoke appreciatively of the trust extended to the lay preacher by Pastor Foss and the ordained staff. In the sacrament of Holy Communion, too, all the members give as well as take the Word and the elements, insofar as the homebound members receive through the hands of fellow receivers the bread and wine consecrated in the congregational gatherings.

When all share in the highest object of the church's life, the communication of the presence of God, rich interrelationships among members ensue. The lay ministry extended across the several congregations of the parish "unifies the churches," said one member. He continued:

> I think we think more of the other churches that are out there than we used to. . . . Before we were more isolated—and those other churches existed—but who ever thought of them? So it has brought more communities a bit more together. . . . We have various joint things at times . . . and so I think there's been some opportunity for interaction between the churches. Sometimes we will go to another church because they're having some event, that we might not have ever gone to before, because we think of them as being a little more as part of our church body and not just another entity out there.

Emerging interpersonal bonds and unity throughout Tri-County were reciprocated in the institutional life of the church. One congregation needed financial help over a two-year period, and the other congregations of the parish, through the Tri-County structure, extended resources to them until they were able to manage on their own. The staff person thought that it "was incredible that they would do that. . . . They made an exception for them." In turn, the staff member mused, "Who knows, maybe the council would make exception again. Any rule that's made can be changed." Thus the enrichment of shared ministry was infusing the institutional structure with a humane ethic.

Vision

An infectious optimism was coursing through all things associated with Tri-County Ministry as empowerment and care fostered a sense of stability and safety in and around the churches. This spirit was abroad even while the cultural trait of caution muted all strong enthusiasms. A fresh "hope of keeping the churches going" was emerging. The new hope was, in the words of one man, to "provide a greater service to the members." The new hope resonated with enduring hopes lodged in the heritages of the individual congregations. One man asked rhetorically:

> You wonder why some of these congregations want to remain open? Go and see their churches. They're very nice. They're small, they're beautiful. Why close them if they can't? So once I got around to seeing them all . . . I said, until it's a natural death, they have some pride there and we need to respect that.

The new vision of cooperation was building upon the visions that had formed and sustained the congregations over time. More than a mere strategy for easing necessary changes, the organic unity of new vision and old in the minds of the people brought deep commitment and social sustenance to the innovative parish.

One participant thought that the cooperative parish helped to make people more adaptable. He said that people "realized that if you don't adapt, you're in trouble." Noting that "they've seen that everywhere else in life around here," he surmised that adaptation within the church should not be a great surprise either. It had been more difficult for some than others, he admitted. Accompanying newfound adaptability was an enduring sense of responsibility and ownership of the church on the part of the laity. In typical fashion, such ownership had previously lodged with resistance to adaptation. Now, there were opportunities and patterns of activity into which members could live their sense of commitment and ownership of the churches, but without defying all innovation.

A sign of adaptation amid persistent commitment to local congregational heritages was the general acceptance of rotation of preachers through the pulpits of Tri-County Ministry. One lay leader remembered complaints about rotation of pastors for worship at the outset. People worried that they would not get to know the pastors. "After the first year or so," he noted, "I didn't hear that anymore. People are happy with what they've got," he concluded. While some began to enjoy the limited variety of preachers, escaping the potential tedium of hearing the same preacher every Sunday, others could no longer use their attachments or dissatisfactions to avoid attendance. "Go down the road 12 miles and catch the other one that you like," advised one member, adding, "See, you can't get off the hook with this model."

The positive direction of personal commitment and ownership was important to this person's overall vision of the church's ministry in the Tri-County area. Narrating a difference before and after Tri-County was in place, a lay leader sensed that members could now express their engagement positively:

> After ten years on the council, I got tired of people coming and saying "Why don't you do this," or "This is wrong; why don't you do this? I don't like the pastor"—you know? So I'd say, "Well, come to the council and speak your piece." Which never happens. Well, when you go through these types of things [the call process and founding of Tri-County] nobody has solutions. And I could see that by putting this package together, it's up to the people. If they want it, fine. If they don't, you go back to what you had. I felt right from the start—I don't know how to describe it—it felt right. Yeah, there were times of trial and tribulation. It felt right because we could get what we wanted. There were going to be no more excuses for not coming to church. Don't like the pastor, whatever those reasons—we had covered. I don't have one pastor now. I have four.

A radical change in vision was germinating within this redirection of deeply held commitments and connection to local congregations. Another lay leader articulated it:

> Some of us are probably beginning to let go of the idea that *the* pastor is the chaplain for this little group. We are beginning to have a broader horizon. We are beginning—again, beginning.

There was still a feeling that Carell Foss was the Cooperstown pastor, the member admitted, but also the people throughout the other congregations knew him as "my pastor." The quality of pastoral care in the Tri-County parish was an important reason that the vision could begin to shift. "Even though these pastors are strung out over a large area," she said, "they are giving far, far better quality, and far greater quantity [of pastoral care] than these people are used to." The organizational ecology of a paid team and invigorated lay leadership was bearing fruit.

The same vision of the Spirit's living presence and work that arose in the planning and development stages became the centerpiece of the growing vision in Tri-County's day-to-day operation. The same farmer who had watched his neighbor sell out the day before was one who could confess the next day:

> So you see, we've had the experience of the Holy Spirit, time and time again. All you got to do is look around. You can see it. It's there. We look for guidance, and so far every time we've looked, it's been there. You have but to ask, so they say.

Vision of the Staff

The staff members share the vision of the people but stand at a different vantage point by virtue of ordained office or special call, and because they are individuals who came originally from outside the Tri-County area. Perhaps the most important element of the staff vision was flexibility and openness to the creativity of God in the laypeople of the parish. Eastern North Dakota Bishop Richard J. Foss explained that the lead pastor, in particular, must be a skilled leader who can take responsibilities seriously each day, but "at night be able to lay his or her head on the pillow and allow that things are out of his or her hands." A gifts minister in Tri-County recognized this quality in Carell Foss. "He does not have the mind structure that says, 'You will color within the lines,'" she remarked. The result was that he and the other staff members were "very good at empowerment."

Matching the laypeople's rootedness in the local communities is the staff's abiding commitment to rural ministry. Carell Foss, for example, worked on a rural ministry committee and traveled to various parts of the country to rural parishes during the farm foreclosures of the 1980s. "What we heard over and over again," he recalled, "was that we want pastors who will come and stay with us, one that will stand by us." The staff members of Tri-County committed themselves to the place where they were called, and learned to cling to its virtues.

"If I were in the ministry right now, I would run to a situation like we've got here," said one layperson. To work with a team, to support one another and discuss problems was a part of the vision of the staff. Sharing and teamwork within the staff went along with the effort to build a supportive network of shared effort and mutual support throughout the parish. Being on a team, another observed, "does enable you to come up with multiple solutions to problems." For rural pastors, who often feel isolated in their work and lives, the cooperative pattern offered both freedom and variety. Carell Foss said he thought that "if you're a pastor with a young family, and you're lonesome, and you feel like you're dealing with everything by yourself—that's hard." Differentiation of tasks and professional support were the only remedies for lonely rural situations.

Within the team and the vision for shared ministry, an important benefit for the office of ordained ministry became evident. While united with the laity in vision and service, those who carry the pastoral office must work hard for the necessary independence of their position. Theologically the ordained must speak prophetically at times, over against the laity. Professionally, an ordained person must serve with an eye to keeping her or his time available and equal to all. In rural communities, often defined by clan, tribe, or folk society, striking a balance between belonging and independence in the pastoral role can be difficult. Pastor Foss picked up on this reality and explained the benefit lodged in a call to Tri-County:

> Rural people are very independent, strong people. They can be very strong in their opinions and can manipulate pastors. If there's three or four of us joined together, that's a little hard! *[chuckles]* I remember one of the people in the congregations said, "Hey, we can't control these people." Well, we don't want to control them, either. But at the same time I don't think we should be manipulated. . . . Our being together, our being united, really makes a big difference.

Healthy differentiation between pastors and people, with an underlying unity of purpose and vision, is a strong benefit to the staff and people of Tri-County Ministry.

Tensions

There are healthy tensions, such as the differentiation in lay and ordained roles; and there are others that tear at the fabric of an institution or a community. The people of Tri-County Ministry articulated an array of concerns, some large and some small, that sometimes harbored both healthy and threatening tensions. Time will tell which tensions the people will accommodate and make routine, and which will become major issues for growth in the institutional life of Tri-County Ministry.

"Travel: it's a big one," stated a farmer when asked about difficulties in the cooperative arrangement. "We are 50, 60 miles across in this parish. . . . Which means our pastors are on the road a lot." Those travels became a real safety concern during harsh winter months. Laity, too, faced long distances for certain programs, and they were once in a while heard to moan about the distances. The purchase of a bus for the youth program was initially a major boost to Tri-County, because the miles to youth gatherings worked a hardship on busy working parents.

The distances created other problems as well. Grace City, at the western edge of the parish, was "kind of the orphan" at times, noted a person from Cooperstown. "They are an isolated community in church and also in school affiliations," the member noted. Carell and Bonnie Foss had a "wonderful way of dealing" with Grace's predicament. They hauled their camper out to Grace City for a couple of weeks or so in the summer, to establish some sense of residence there. That practice worked wonders, but the distance lengthened during the harsh winter months.

Another problem, basically attributable to a small staff trying to cover a large geographical area, was that the staff sometimes did not hear of a pastoral need until after its acute phase. "The hardest thing," said Bonnie Foss, "is knowing what's going on everywhere." She was sad that "some people have gotten sick and been to the hospital and gotten home before we've found out." Precautions were in place to prevent that from happening. "Shepherds" were designated in each of the congregations, "and the duty of the shepherd is to let us know if someone becomes ill and is hospitalized, so that we can go visit them." Sometimes the system didn't keep up with the needs, however. "That's the most frustrating part," Bonnie Foss said, ". . . not hearing about someone during their time of crisis." It seemed to happen in the four towns where a pastor did not reside. An important ministry opportunity was missed at those crucial times, she recognized, and so the staff continued to struggle against the distance.

For many of the laity a continuing tension was the perceived lack of pastoral presence, particularly in the communities where a parsonage stood empty. The one-pastor-one-church norm lived on in personal expectations of many people, even after they had accepted the new vision of the cooperative ministry and lay ministry. "Even now," after five years, said one staff member, "it's hard for people to get past that 'my pastor' feeling.

They tend to want an ownership of the pastor that lives in their town." Part of this sentiment arose from the personal dimension, as the area's physician explained:

> When you have a pastor all alone, there's that feeling of "your pastor"; you have a close relationship with that person. When you call, you always know whom you're going to get. . . . In the current program, if you need somebody, there's a possibility that you're not going to know who you're going to get. . . . And I think that's at times a little bit of a problem.

For example, he said he'd seen family members of a deceased loved one have to ponder and decide whom they would call. "So I think there's a little less personal relationship at times." However, the doctor also recognized that "you at least know that it's pretty likely that there *is* going to be somebody" for pastoral ministry at all times. In a single pastorate, the one pastor could be unavailable at certain emergency times anyway. Therefore, he surmised, "the disadvantage is offset by advantage."

The desire for parsonage residency had a community dimension beyond the personal relationships to a particular pastor. In a context where other institutions were consolidating away from the area, an occupied parsonage could be a rallying symbol for people who hope to sustain their small community. The intimate tie between pastoral presence and parsonage residence made the fact that the Tri-County Council oversaw parsonages along with clergy finances seem wise. An empty parsonage could be a sore spot remaining after the Tri-County Council had worked through the difficulties of assembling the calls to a team. When an intern was unavailable, or where a clergy couple served in place of two unrelated pastors, Tri-County found itself making some difficult negotiations with pastors and congregations, that would affect the communities and area they served.

The desire for congregational autonomy has similar community-wide significance, beyond the personal level of ownership. In turn, another tension persists in Tri-County between control of the parish council and the local congregational councils. One layperson explained:

> I don't think any of the churches around here wants to have any one of the other churches telling them what they should be doing. I think they're still very much autonomous, even if they do feel a

stronger bond of unity. I think it's important that we increase this feeling. But I don't see in the future that any one of these churches is going to feel that they should now be controlled by the other churches. That's not the background of these churches, or the people. They're very self-reliant people. . . . They try to hang on to these little churches and schools.

To maintain the balance between coordinated common effort and congregational independence, the architects of the Tri-County structure developed fair processes, examined below in the discussion of "Why it Works." The centripetal pull of congregational autonomy was well illustrated, however, about a year and a half into the cooperative, when one congregation could not meet the agreed-upon apportionment for pastoral services and parish programming. The council asked if it had done a stewardship campaign or made efforts to raise the offerings needed, and it had not. "Well then, how can we give you any special favors?" reasoned one council member. The one congregation wanted a budget reduction to accommodate its own situation. "I'm sorry," responded one later; "we all went in there with our eyes open." Then the representatives of that congregation indulged themselves in some speculation that maybe they would have to go on their own, separating from Tri-County Ministry. The chairperson of that time later recalled:

I said, "Fine. That's why we have the mechanics in place so you can withdraw if that's what your congregation [wants to do]." No, they got busy. Tri-County had to subsidize them that second year and third year so they could get their ducks in a row and take a hard look at this, and rally their own members who weren't coming and weren't giving.

One council member drew a lesson from the experience. "It's very easy to become sympathetic" to those who balk at cooperative commitments, this member observed. This person believed that there was sympathy and support in the actions the Tri-County council took at that time, because Tri-County was doing what it could realistically to keep the individual congregations strong together. After all, this was an important part of Tri-County's mission, "to help them stay open," as one put it. But that commitment of the whole to the individual parts could not be extended to the detriment of the whole. The commitment was there, said one council member, but "don't bleed it, either, to your advantage. That's not what this is about."

Normally in Tri-County the needs and wants of individual congregations could be accommodated, with the end result that the cluster of congregations making up Tri-County Ministry began to enjoy individual vitality in
tandem with intercongregational commitments. For example, there was a
variety of worship experiences across the parish. Each congregation had its
own order of worship, hymnals, and service books, ranging from main-
stream Lutheran traditions to informal evangelical and contemporary practices. For the staff, rotating through the congregations for worship leadership, the variety meant potential confusion in coping with variant practices
from Sunday to Sunday. A unified worship bulletin was just a dream at the
time of this study. However, through fine coordination the staff was accommo-
dating congregational traditions and preferences in worship, within the broader
rubrics of the Christian, Lutheran, and Presbyterian liturgical traditions.

Meeting the breadth of congregational practices and needs raised the
issues of overextension of staff and lay leadership. "The downside in our
case," stated a leader, "is too much to do." An additional staff member
would help a lot, he said. "There's still a great demand" for all the ministries
of the parish, even though they had "broken that down a little bit." For the
pastors, the extensive needs meant that evenings got totally booked between meetings and calls. Carell Foss stated, "I don't think a young pastor
with family can do that." If the cooperative parish arrangement were to
relieve staff overextension, a tension endemic to church work in general, it
would require a slightly larger team than Tri-County had.

Why It Works

Tensions can call forth creativity and thus be helpful in spurring growth.
While some of the tensions remained problematic, there was a strong sense
among the members and staff of Tri-County Ministry that the cooperative
parish arrangement was working well. The members articulated a number of
specific factors that they thought were contributing to Tri-County's success.

Fair representation and minimal governance fostered political harmony
in Tri-County Ministry. Tri-County Council consists of two representatives
from each congregation. "Whether you are the largest or not, you have
equal power," noted Carell Foss. "If you were to adjust the voice in management according to the size of congregations," he speculated, "I think
there would be some upsetting." The two representatives share a single

vote in the council. One of the designers of the system explained the reasons:

> If one member of that two-member team was absent, they could
> still vote. The second reason is that those two people can confer,
> so it's not one person saying, "Oh, I feel that way." Thirdly, I knew
> that a lot of small churches . . . could look at the largest church
> and say, "Well, you're the big kid on the block, and you're going to
> get your way, and you're going to muscle your way, and we're just
> going to be tipped over." Let's start fair from the beginning and
> say, "Nope, we feel for you people. You have a voice." And I also
> believe that . . . yeah, the small churches could gang up on the big
> one, but I really don't think that would ever happen because you're
> there for the right reasons.

Not leaving everything to the better motives just cited, another aspect of the Tri-County system of governance balanced power between the congregations: congregational referendum.

Decision-making in Tri-County was "a sort of referendum," noted one member. "They decide at the Tri-County Council and bring it back to the local church councils, such as budget and major decisions like that." Notwithstanding the tensions of congregational autonomy that the system preserves, local involvement is balanced with the central influence that some leaders might achieve through the Tri-County Council votes. In short, "Tri-County proposes, and the local council disposes," said one observer with a laugh. If the congregational councils say no, then Tri-County Council goes "back to the drawing board." So far, the democratic confederation was working well, as another explained:

> We are equally represented, just like the U.S. Senate. These people
> elect their leaders on that council. So if [Tri-County Council]
> chooses a leader from [Trinity, the largest congregation], we are
> not stuffing the ballot boxes. And the interesting thing is that with
> our system of representation, we have to make the smallest con-
> gregations happy, because if they are not satisfied, then it's all
> scrapped. Perhaps they are harder to please than the big one. On
> the other hand, they are very aware. These congregations with
> the tiny memberships are aware that this is it; they'd better hang

on to this, because it's costing them less than it would cost them in another arrangement.

The system for making decisions at least had the virtue of keeping people involved with determining their own circumstances, so far as that was possible for anyone. Such practice was consistent with the preservation and stimulation of lay leadership in Tri-County Ministry.

Stimulation of lay ownership, and lay responsibility in relation to the real challenges of the church's institutional life, were additional reasons that Tri-County was working well. One leader explained how lay ownership was reshaped in Tri-County from passive attachment to one pastor as a service provider to active investment in the partnership of ministry:

> I think we broke that Lutheran selfishness that maybe this part of the country experiences. "I want my own pastor, I want my own church and I want him [or her] to come to my house, and why isn't he [or she] at my cousin's funeral, and why this—because it's me." We've broken that because in this case it was evident that I have four pastors now. Well, how am I going to get to meet them? I have to make an effort. I have to meet them 50 percent of the way. I can't expect all four of them to cater to this ownership that we Lutherans have been brought up with. In this case, to make it better, we had to reach out, rather than sit in the same pew in the same Sunday and expect the pastor to come to shake my hand. I think we've broken that a little bit and gotten people to venture out and say, "I have to contribute here because it's good." I gain more the more I contribute.

Personal effort within the parish ministry yielded the benefits of communal attachments to others besides the pastors, the same person argued. He thought the removal of the passive option in relationships with pastors had "helped the volunteer aspect a little bit, too."

Tri-County worked well partly because it used budding lay engagement in efficient and rewarding ways. For example, council meetings in Tri-County, after emerging from initial planning stages, were not as long as Trinity's own council meetings used to be. "We don't come to talk about the whole thing," said one chairperson. Participants were encouraged to "make a recommendation, so we can act on it." Efficiency in procedures called people to accountability but also rewarded their efforts with a sense of accomplishment.

The very existence of a Tri-County Council was a boon to the attitudes of some small-church leaders. While carrying responsibilities for an individual congregation's management, it was encouraging to know that one was not alone. Meanwhile, "the benefits maybe are going to be manifold because those 25 who now do get together [at a small church] will feel better about doing it." The small-church gathering was "providing the opportunity for individual growth," and Tri-County was working well in that it supported and tapped the energy and commitment that those small units sustained.

Meanwhile, the presence of the large church in the cooperative was important for Tri-County to work well. Trinity in Cooperstown was an anchor for the cooperative parish, especially in its stable base of human and financial resources. Trinity was capable of supporting its own pastor and some additional staff. The people of Trinity entered the cooperative for the benefits of a full staff ministry, which they could not quite afford on their own. "Trinity did not think of themselves as being noble," remarked one person. "They said, 'We want this because we can get more this way.' So they looked at it from the standpoint that they were thinking of themselves, but really *[laughs]*, they were being noble." The interviewee spoke for many when she said simply, "We couldn't do it without them. We really need to have one large church. You need that financial base to do it." She doubted what the outcome would have been without Trinity: "If you have a bunch of little churches, I'm not sure you could do it."

Trinity people were "used to having a pastor here every day all the time." In Tri-County Ministry, the lead pastor resided in the parsonage next to Trinity, Cooperstown. There was a residual sense that the lead pastor filled the same shoes Trinity pastors had prior to Tri-County. However, the lead pastor served all the congregations of Tri-County, and Trinity had rotation in worship leadership and in other pastoral services. While the difference in day-to-day experience for Trinity is minimal, "they just don't have [a pastor] here every day all the time because they need to be in other places," said a staff member. Therefore, "if any feel the loss of what they had in terms of a pastor on site all the time, it would be them." Yet there was general satisfaction in Trinity thus far.

The skill and aptitude of the lead pastor, Carell Foss, and his wife, Bonnie, were undoubtedly major reasons that Trinity was content and Tri-County Ministry was working overall. Meanwhile, the benefits of serving on a pastoral team are one answer to the question of why Tri-County works well. "In this case," said one layperson, "everybody has a niche. And that older pastor doesn't have to be the youth pastor. . . . Or that young pastor, to go and visit with the elderly might be a lot harder for him early in his [or her] career." Each pastor still did a little of all activities, but "you can be a specialist" while also being "a generalist," to build skills in ministry. Still, the team of pastors needed vision, direction, and leadership from a central figure. Carell Foss had provided that, and his own ministry was inextricably bound up with the success of Tri-County Ministry as a whole.

Future

As people turned their thoughts toward the future, the inevitable retirement of the lead pastor and the task of finding a successor loomed. At the time of the study, no one, including Carell and Bonnie Foss, was anticipating the retirement just yet. However, Bonnie Foss was retiring from her job as coordinator, and by 1999, Pastor Foss had announced his coming retirement, too. Asked about finding a suitable replacement for the lead pastor, lay and clergy alike responded with hopefulness that God would provide the "right" person at the right time. Beyond such hopes, the people had not formulated in their minds yet the shape of the crucial task of moving from the first lead pastor to the first successor. "My only fear," voiced Carell Foss, "would be if they cut back on staff to where they work people too hard."

Attracting staff to a rural area and an innovative ministry was a wider concern among laity and staff members who looked to the future. A farmer observed:

> I think it's difficult to get pastors into this type of area where, number one, it's very rural and somewhat isolated; number two, the remuneration is not wonderful; and, number three, they can't just comfortably slip into one spot and just work with one group of people. Suddenly they're running all over three counties and eight churches and preaching here and running out the door around the corner to the Presbyterian church. To some people that seems like a real opportunity, but for others that looks like a real job. I think it's tough to get people who are made for that. So I think the

biggest threat to the coalition is the continued availability of pastors who can provide that kind of service.

Many agreed that the internship program at Tri-County was a potential feeder for parish leadership and rural ministry overall. "We're planting some ground here for the new pastor of the future to be in rural ministry," said one layperson. She thought that with the training of interns in Tri-County, "we've really hit on something that's strong for the future of the ELCA." The people of Tri-County, with an exciting and effective model, were able to teach seminarians that "it's not all bad out here" in a rural parish. Another person speculated that some interns would want to come back, and some would perhaps "get scared and never come back," but the experience "would probably be a source of future pastors for rural ministry." So far the interns have had positive experiences.

The context to which ordained and professional leaders would be called would likely be an unstable one. "We have to be realistic," cautioned one lay leader, because the plight of the area was "just due to demographics and agricultural changes—things that are beyond our control." The people of Tri-County were divided in their opinion of whether some churches would close as a result of declining population and consolidation in farming. Many focused on the fact that "some of the churches are very small," concluding that "there will be one or two that in the future will close." The key reason, according to some, would be that "it will be very difficult to send a pastor to a church for ten people," referring to a diminished worship attendance. Others liked to believe that the future admitted of more possibilities than the demographics and economic trends indicated. There could be four churches in Tri-County in future years, or there could be 12, one woman believed. Her vision, shared by others, was "that eventually this will be the place to be," as population in search of open spaces and clean living would one day arrive.

Speculations about closing churches led to questions of consolidation of congregations. Would there ever come a day when Tri-County would hold a unified budget, dispensed for several worship sites? One person thought that would not happen, because:

One of the keys to our success is that [the people] still feel that they have control over their own church. They still can decide a lot of church matters on their own. The church [building] is still owned by their church. But we've taken and relieved some of the pressure from them.

Another person concluded that if the "worst-case scenario" did come about, and "one or two happen to close due to people or financial reasons," then "there is a sister church that they can go to." Although in church closings it is most common for bereaved members not to transfer their allegiances to a neighboring congregation, Tri-County had created the context of relationship to foster the transfer, a lay leader believed. "The barriers have broken down now so that when [closing] does take place, if it needs to, it's much easier to drive down the road 20 miles or 12 miles and see those people because you've mingled with them prior to this in different settings." Moreover, "there's a common thread there" in the shared mission of Tri-County Ministry.

Financial decline was a looming threat even if demographics did not cause demise. Lay leaders of Tri-County were pushing remedial action against draining resources. "We've taken some steps to protect [financial viability] by setting up some foundations," reported one. "The money that's in those foundations can be invested and spun off to subsidize, so our members don't have to keep taking increases." Since Tri-County started on the promise that it wouldn't be any more expensive than independent operation of congregations, the Tri-County leaders deemed the continual increase in the Tri-County budget to be a serious problem. In five years, it had increased by more than $30,000. In the face of the political challenge of passing the budget each year, the financial leaders of the parish had "risen to the occasion" with the plan for endowments, "because they like what they see" in Tri-County programming and ministry. "We may be at the top end" of demographics and financial resources, they reasoned, because of declining births and increasing age. "If we can subsidize this now by investments," one leader explained, "that will give it some stability."

Whether they were to expand or contract financially and demographically, the people of Tri-County said they hoped for "spiritual growth," continuing increase in fellowship and relationships in the parish, and evangelism to neighbors (most of whom were inactive members of churches). While one could hope for "some nice clean industry that employs a lot of people" to come into the area and solve demographic and financial problems, one person said her "hunch is that the answer is not that." Rather, she reflected, vitality lies "in our spiritual life, in our growth as individuals and as members of the body of Christ working together." She believed that "we need somehow to become convinced, become stricken as it were." Another hoped that spiritual conviction would foster "interaction between the churches" and "create a stronger bond" between the congregations. Many hoped that such vitality in the churches would spill over into the local communities, particularly in evangelism to inactive members. One lay leader framed the situation by saying "OK, the model works; there's no excuses" for staying away from church. A concerted ministry to "inactives" was "probably how things are going to continue" in Tri-County Ministry, said Carell Foss. Beyond that, he hoped for community outreach in the form of a nursing-home chaplain and a locally resident family therapist. Such positions could be supported partly by Tri-County, and rounded out to viable part-time or full-time positions by Lutheran Social Services or the local nursing home. The counselor in particular could influence the quality of life in the area, because people were in great need of conflict resolution and related services, but largely resisted traveling for services to larger towns outside the immediate area.

Local complacency was a perceived internal threat to the Tri-County parish itself. In the beginning days "a crisis" caused people "to sit up and take notice," said one founding lay leader. The perception after five years was "It's working now, and everything's fine." Another person explained that "the danger gets to be, pretty soon, we've got enough experience under our belts, and we think we can make this thing run by ourselves." That "could be a pitfall," he believed, because "you've got to trust the Holy Spirit is going to make it go."

In a similar vein, the generations of Tri-County Council leaders who come after the founding generation might naturally succumb to complacency. A farmer explained:

> The danger is that the people who are rotating through after us didn't go through the original struggles. They didn't go through the building. They haven't had to fight tooth and nail to make it go. Do they appreciate what they've got? But that's the way it is whenever you build anything. That's the way it is on a farm. You're responsible for your own operation. You've got to make it go, and if you don't, you're out of business.

Just as in any church, explained another founder, "if you don't have a project going, you kind of lose focus." He declared that "you need goals to keep people on track with purpose and meaning," and that goal maintenance was "leadership's responsibility." If they were not doing that, then "there's risk." This leader cautioned that "we haven't wanted to talk about that in the past, because, well, everybody's content." People believed that "as long as we've got a pastor, we're okay." Complacency might lead to avoidance of the pressing mission and outreach needs, and denial of demographic and financial trends.

Tri-County Ministry stood on the verge of the challenging transfer of leadership from the successful first generation to an as-yet-untried second generation. This was true in both lay leadership and paid staff. The sense of satisfaction over the general health and vitality of the cooperative parish, starkly contrasting to contextual decline in North Dakota, was palpable to the authors of this study during their 1997 visits. Tensions in the present and threats in the future notwithstanding, the people of Tri-County Ministry were working to envision a future that would meet the challenges and opportunities, rather than anticipating disintegration of the innovative mission strategy. Asked if the congregations, which retain a great deal of autonomy, would pull away from Tri-County over tensions or disagreements about strategies for the future, one layperson laughed and said:

> Like, we can get married because we can always get divorced later? I don't think that our feeling is that. In the back of our mind we know that we're not . . . *[pause]* It could happen. It could split and reorganize and go back to being a one-point parish. But after we have been involved with the other congregations, we have benefited from our associations with the other people.

Therefore, Tri-County Ministry would probably continue to express the integral unity of the whole church, in lively tension with the energy of local assemblies, for the benefit of a hard-pressed area. Drawing its own household into a communal formation, the church through Tri-County was now poised to foster community on the wide-open plains.

CHAPTER 2

North Central Cluster, West Virginia

North Central Cluster

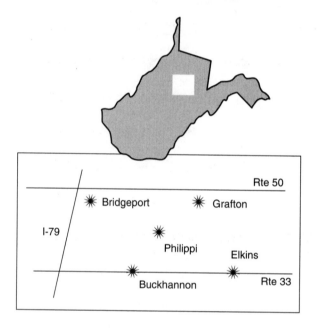

THE NORTH CENTRAL CLUSTER

Episcopal Diocese of West Virginia, Episcopal Church

Headquarters: Bridgeport, West Virginia

Missioner: The Rev. Kelly Marshall

Cooperative makeup: four Episcopal congregations

Birthdate: 1990, reorganized 1996

Special Ministries: Lay pastoral visitation

Staff: Missioner (full-time, all other staff part-time),
local "Canon 9 priest," two retired priests, part-time priest,
secretary, and lay administrator

West Virginia

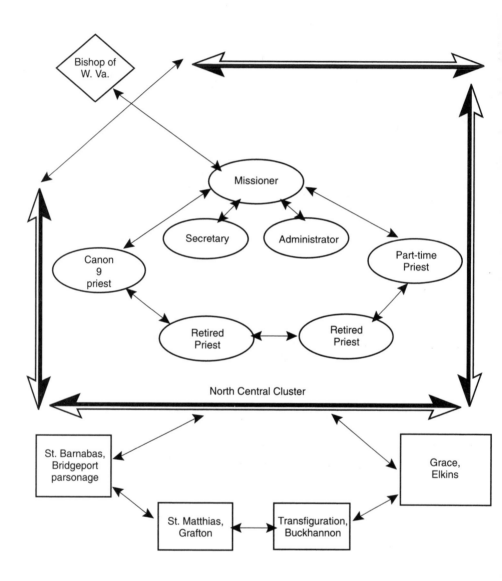

North Central Cluster, West Virginia

When 15 to 35 people gathered to worship in each of the four congregations of the North Central Cluster in West Virginia in 1997, they knew they were staking a basic claim that the church, as they had known it, would survive in their communities. Three of the four were the sole Episcopal congregations in their county-seat towns. The four were Grace Church in Elkins, St. Matthias in Grafton, Transfiguration in Buckhannon, and St. Barnabas in Bridgeport. A county in the middle of the four congregations lost its Episcopal congregation to membership attrition. Diminished membership and finances in the congregations matched population decline and economic hardship in the context. Lay and ordained members of the North Central Cluster were in the serious throes of a fight for their lives—at least the lives of their small communities of faith. The North Central Cluster was a bottom-line effort to turn their institutional fortunes around.

The pastoral staff spoke often of maintaining "eucharistic presence" in the north-central region of West Virginia through the clustered congregations. The phrase "eucharistic presence" harbored a collection of meanings, including especially the regular administration of the sacrament of Holy Communion according to the rites of the Episcopal Church, part of the worldwide Anglican Communion. "Eucharistic presence" also evoked the full range of basic Christian ministry: preaching and teaching; formation and growth of believers in the traditions of the church; and sound pastoral care available from cradle to grave.

Eucharistic presence and mere survival were juxtaposed in the North Central Cluster. Accordingly, a hopeful and exciting sense of mission competed with a debilitating survival mentality in the day-to-day world of both laity and clergy. In the initial stages of cluster formation, the aches and pains of changing institutional patterns were often indistinguishable from the newer structural issues germane to clustering. A glimpse of congregational experience in the North Central Cluster in 1997 is a peek into both the stresses and the budding promise of cooperative ministry in its earliest stages. The hard demographic and economic issues of the West Virginia context highlight the danger the clustering congregations have faced, but also frame how generous the benefits of cluster success might be.

Context

A high Appalachian plateau extends over the north-central region of West Virginia. Spruce Knob, the highest peak in West Virginia, displays its 4,863 feet on the eastern edge of the North Central Cluster of the Episcopal diocese. An undulating landscape of prominent summits, rolling hills, and sharp valleys create the fabled ridges and "hollers" of Appalachian lore. "Hollers" are small valleys rimmed on three sides by steep inclines, sites of geographic and cultural separation even in contemporary times. Meanwhile, the open valleys and riverbeds have been the arteries of industrialization and immigration, leading to the area's ethnic diversity. Historic themes of the American frontier, the Civil War, early labor movements and the independent mountaineer mingle with contemporary trends of exurban development, chronic poverty, and economic exploitation of natural and human communities.

The Rev. Kelly Marshall, the missioner of the North Central Cluster, wound his way for miles and miles over the rolling landscape among four congregations that served eight counties. The North Central Cluster was not only far-flung geographically; it was as variegated in community contexts as in landscape features. A typical morning found Father Marshall embarking from his home in Bridgeport, a suburban-style developing area booming from industrial expansion and construction of a new Federal Bureau of Investigation complex. Viewed locally, Bridgeport was a suburb of the small city of Clarksburg, West Virginia; but regionally it was growing in relation to Pittsburgh, Pennsylvania, 100 miles to the north, and Washington, D.C., over the mountains to the east. Interstate highways running north-south and east-west had eased Bridgeport's emergence, and a planned new highway would similarly cut through the mountains and open the southern portion of the North Central Cluster's territory to Interstate 81 and the Washington, D.C. megalopolis. For the time being, however, Father

Marshall's daily journeys throughout his parish took him roundabout on winding lanes, through wooden covered bridges and around hairpin mountain curves.

At Bridgeport, Kelly Marshall worked in a modern structure nestled on the edge of established housing developments, sprawling malls, and superstores. The location, parking, and architecture of St. Barnabas Church were inviting and accessible. The congregation's small size defied its potential, as is the case with so many recent mission starts that do not transcend their cozy beginning stages. (Shortly after the time of this study, the Bridgeport church left the North Central Cluster, and became a partner with the nearby congregation of Clarksburg.)

Father Marshall would drive back in time, as it were, as he worked his way over to Grafton on old U.S. Route 50. The telltale icon of Grafton's history was its hulking and empty B&O Railroad Hotel, towering over its tiny and increasingly vacant downtown area. Nestled in a gap where the Tygart River flows toward the Monongahela, Grafton was originally an important railroad hub in the days of Abraham Lincoln and other east-west travelers of the mid-19th century. Birthplace of Mother's Day, Grafton was the home base of Anna Jarvis's campaign for peace, temperance, and social improvement. The model community of the 19th and early 20th centuries became, however, a passed-over town. The interstates were built to the west and north of Grafton, and as automobiles replaced railroads, Grafton lost its strategic location. Startling poverty and pervasive lack of opportunity were most evident in today's Grafton, even while a few affluent people took advantage of the Tygart Lake recreational area on Grafton's south side.

Father Marshall would reach Saint Matthias Church on the main street of Grafton, and ascend 50 feet of concrete steps to reach the outdoor stoop of the chapel-size church. Almost the same distance of steps rose behind the church on its steep lot to the narrow "rear" street. The church's physical setting mirrored its long-standing isolation and self-sufficiency. Yet, this congregation, too, was a participant in the cluster, and saw its survival and its ability to have a resident priest tied to the cluster.

Traveling toward the south during his frequent journeys, Father Marshall passed through Barbour County and the town of Philippi. The Episcopal parish in Philippi closed a few years before Father Marshall's arrival, leaving the college town and county seat, as well as Barbour County, to be served by the other congregations of the cluster. The loss of the Philippi parish is a fresh memory and a vivid reminder to the other congregations of the plight that threatens them. One elder parishioner commented on the liturgy of closing held at the Philippi church:

> We went over to Philippi when they had the closing. I'd never seen a closing of a church before. And oh, it was so sad; you know they just stripped everything. And I said, "You know, that could happen to us."

Seeing closure was so hard for one member that he said, "It's like it's a piece of you and it's over and it's finished." Another noticed that the refugees of closures are often lost to church or at least to the denomination involved:

> If you close any one of [the cluster congregations], you really have displaced the people. We closed the church in Philippi, and I don't know as we've had just one husband and wife come here. . . . I don't know what happened to the rest of those people up there. We didn't retain much of what we had. If that happened here [a neighboring congregation], I think we'd see some fallout.

The stakes were high for the parishes entering into a cooperative. The difficulties of congregational survival are well-recognized in mission literature, but few understand the heartfelt issues of those who have experienced the grief and loss of church closures in their own and neighboring congregations. Survival for small churches is not an abstract issue in cooperatives as it is in mission resources that glibly accept or even encourage church closures. Where it has happened, closure is the wolf at the door.

The tenor of possibilities rose in a hopeful strain, nevertheless, as Father Marshall moved further southward to the small but active congregations in Buckhannon and Elkins. These were college towns like Philippi, with Elkins being recognized beyond West Virginia as an Appalachian cultural center. They, with Philippi, had social and economic potential that had escaped Grafton. Each congregation had a sense of its distinctive ministry in its community, and its own strong identity as a congregation. A modernized highway encouraged exchange between Buckhannon and Elkins and promised a future of commerce with the Washington area across the Appalachians.

At the same time, these towns remain rather isolated in many respects. As one staff member put it:

> If you live in Elkins, West Virginia, you are committed to living in
> Elkins, West Virginia. You don't come there by accident; it's not a
> way-station. It's not a suburb. If you make it through one winter,
> you're real committed. You're hours from an airport; you're hours
> from shopping. So you've got a real sense of "I'm here and I'm
> gonna make sure Elkins is home."

Within the geography of the cluster, Elkins and Buckhannon constituted the
southern tier and were about an hour's drive from either of the northern
partners. In turn, Father Marshall said that his car was his office, and he
spent more time in it than anywhere else. His travels and work were the
most tangible sign of the congregations' relatedness. Otherwise, they were
segmented in their very different community contexts and separate counties. Only Buckhannon and Elkins shared a similarity of type, in neighboring
counties. But Grafton was a world and an age away, while Bridgeport was
swept into the vanguard of the dominant market economy and consumer
culture.

In patterns of association, from informal crossovers at shopping sites
and recreational opportunities, to formal memberships in institutions, the
residents of the four communities were almost completely distinct. Some
family and lifestyle patterns overlapped, and hence a few from the closed
congregation in Philippi joined in Buckhannon or Grafton. But even the new
highways had not meshed the four distinctive communities.

Two contextual realities are competing with one another in north-central West Virginia. They are evident in parishioners' attitudes about getting
together for cluster activities and meetings. An age-old reality is that of
separate communities and separate parishes. The majority of older members in the cluster, living in this reality, view the driving distances between
communities, especially in rough West Virginia winters, as inordinate. On
the other hand, those whose past or present is enmeshed in our time with
the dominant culture of North America view the four communities in five
counties as close together. Driving from Elkins to Bridgeport for shopping
or a restaurant meal is routine, and traveling the same distance for a church
meeting is no sacrifice.

Deeper issues than the physical distances between communities are
the painful social and personal transitions born of a century's social change.
One member of the cluster described the struggle of a beloved community
elder with the changes in one of the towns of the cluster:

One of the women who's 90 years old, her husband's family settled that town. They started the bank; they started the hospital; they gave their land and homes to the college. She hates [certain changes], and she's had a terrible time. Because the bank is different: they tore down the old building and built a new one; the same thing with the hospital. The home she lived in when she was brought here as a bride from New York is now an inn. There's just one thing after another that's losing its identity.

The competing realities of North America, dominant globalized culture, and resistant local cultures, form the context of the North Central Cluster of the Diocese of West Virginia. A visionary ecclesiological model and a missioner named Kelly Marshall move between the two contextual realities and weave a larger whole, a kingdom of God's presence through the ministry of the church of Jesus Christ. It was that churchly reality that two listeners, the authors of this book, came to witness in West Virginia in 1997.

Development

Bishop John H. Smith came to the Episcopal Diocese of West Virginia in 1989 with a vision for "Cluster Ministry." Experienced with small-church ministry in Maine and Vermont, Bishop Smith provided the opportunities and guidance for cluster ministries throughout his entire diocese. The churches of the North Central Cluster were not completely inexperienced in intercongregational arrangements. Yoked parishes of various configurations were a strategy for providing pastoral service throughout the area. In Buckhannon, priests who were teaching at the local college had served the parish part-time. Beginning in 1985, the congregations began experimenting with greater levels of cooperation, with a predecessor called the Crescent Parish giving way in 1990 to the North Central Cluster. Bishop Smith nurtured a shift in perspective, subtly but firmly changing the parameters of intercongregational arrangements from survival strategies to a missional posture.

Bishop Smith expressed his full vision for cooperative ministries in *Cluster Ministry: A Faithful Response to Change.* After seven years of cluster ministries in the diocese, the bishop wrote that there was

a new sense of hope, a developing of baptismal ministry, a growing ownership in and responsibility for mission and a tremendous
improvement in self-esteem among the congregations involved in
the cluster.[1]

In short, the bishop envisioned a "shift . . . from survival or maintenance to mission" that "lies at the heart of Jesus' teaching." Grounding
strategy in a theological appreciation of the mission of small churches, and
a sociological grasp of current challenges for congregations, he went on to
discuss the practical issues of forming clusters. The bishop maintained an
evolutionary perspective over the "living organisms" that were clusters in
his diocese. He emphasized that he would force no congregation into a
cluster, but he recognized that within the pain of hard changes individuals in
congregations would continue to deny that they had choices and would
blame diocese, bishop, or circumstances. On the positive side, clusters encouraged covenanted relationships at many levels, not least a covenant with
God that would lead congregations and individuals into vibrant mission. Again
commenting on seven years of experience, Bishop Smith held:

Clusters have helped congregations to move beyond survival mentality and beyond the co-dependency that has often been created
between congregations and the diocese.[2]

The North Central Cluster began the journey in the direction indicated by
Bishop Smith shortly after his arrival in the diocese. The cluster emerged
from former intercongregational arrangements, and was reorganized a number of times before what Smith characterized as "a dramatic breakthrough
in the spring of 1996."[3] In that year, with pastoral vacancies in all sites:

the congregations consciously moved from the chaplaincy model
or consumer model of church in which the church exists for the
benefit of its members to a missional model of church.[4]

The cluster called Kelly Marshall as missioner, and assembled a pastoral
staff that included some retired and part-time priests, and a layperson who
was becoming a "local canon priest."

At the center of the regional ministry strategy was the identification,
training, and ordination of local candidates for the priesthood. Under Canon 9

of the Episcopal Church's canon law, a diocese in a missionary setting is able to ordain bivocational clergy who have been called, educated, and prepared for ordination within the local diocese rather than in a traditional seminary setting. The canon allows, for example, a local leader to develop naturally into a parish priest for her or his own area, under the aegis of the diocesan bishop. While the Canon 9 priest is eventually differentiated from the laity by ordination, the accessibility of the office of ministry in a local setting in fact honors and elevates the importance of all lay ministers in that place. The Canon 9 option fosters asset development in local settings, and works against the ordained ministry being sequestered in the hands of those who can muster the financial resources for a traditional seminary education.

Meanwhile, Father Marshall's work in the reformed cluster had a unifying and normalizing effect on the congregations and parishioners. After a year in an interim status, Marshall accepted the call to be missioner. One parishioner remembered:

> The whole cluster felt renewed when Kelly agreed to become our priest. . . . I know that everyone was just thrilled, and we had been given a second chance to grow and prosper. I think we had a renewed commitment to work together because of this. You know, it was a rebirthing. And we still do very much want it to work.

The opportunities of Bishop Smith's vision were budding.

The transitions in pastoral staff and clustering arrangements were nearly devastating for the congregations, however. Uncertainty and the normal trials of transitions exacerbated the problems of developing trust, vision, and ownership among members. "It just seems like there has been constant change in the cluster," remarked one lay leader, and "that, I think, has generally caused problems." A staff member characterized the congregations as "abused children" in a dysfunctional family. Although this staff member was also referring to struggles that did not necessarily arise from clustering efforts, the protean landscape of clustering contributed to a certain bewilderment and withdrawal in the clustered congregations. A particularly rough time ensued when two priests shared cluster direction, and could not collaborate. The one in the northern tier and the one in the south conflicted in perspectives and values across their geographical divide. The conflicting leaders were like fighting parents, a staff member said. Continuing the family metaphor, she said that "while the marriage [of the congregations into a cluster] took place with [congregational] consent, the children were not the decision makers."

The cluster had to start at "ground zero" when the squabbling priests departed and Father Marshall arrived. In this light, a staff member characterized the cluster as solely a survival mechanism, and implied that its positive characteristics were by-products. When you "climb into a lifeboat," the staff member said, "there's warmth; there's companionship; there's people to pull the oars." But "we climbed in for survival." Fighting clergy and stressful transitions made it difficult to rise above the level of survival mechanisms.

Such experience presents the challenge to deepen relationships to a level of truly trusting one another. The cohesiveness of a lifeboat community easily breaks down. A lay leader briefly narrated what it was like:

> Ah, it took a long time to build trust. You had the old Crescent Parish, which had a certain way of doing things and wanted to remain that way. And you had three congregations coming into that who really didn't feel they were locked into that. A lot of times the priests were involved and didn't handle it as well as they could have. You had two congregations siding with this priest or another. And those two priests weren't getting along together.

Another parishioner spoke of the congregations being "abused, threatened, harassed" in direct relationship to the challenge of the cluster budget, which he felt was too large and difficult for small churches. The congregations, he said, can only raise about half of the "gigantic budget" (Actually, the total budget at the time of this study was $90,000; the congregations raised $50,000; and Grafton by itself was responsible for $6,000). "We are expected to act like a big church," he complained. Moreover, "priests come here with no guidelines for working with a small church," and consequently perpetuate the expectations that would be more appropriate to a large church. Most others, however, saw the cluster budget as a relief for individual church finances, as another lay leader said:

> When we weren't a cluster it was $54,000 to run this church a year, and now we're doing it for [$45,000]. So if you don't like any of the rest of the things that are associated with the cluster, you at least know that we've been able to stay alive at less cost.

Many others cited the financial benefit of clustering, and thus the complaint above, while questionable substantively, is primarily a sign of the emotional struggle of committing to cluster mission.

The very beginning of clustering efforts was an affront to many people. "The low point had to be when we first joined" the cluster, recalled one member from Elkins, "because we were going from parish status back to mission status." In the Episcopal Church, "parish status" meant full financial sufficiency and the right to call one's own rector, while "mission status" meant that a congregation was financially dependent on the diocese and the bishop functioned as rector. Established parish status was a goal long promoted by diocesan efforts of past decades, and long a goal of individual congregations. Some parishioners were not energized by a vision of returning to frontier and early-church models of mission, in part because they saw it as a lapse in progress. The mission model of Bishop Smith did not allow dependency in either mission status or parish status, but the many years of promotion of the parish status as the mark of success obscured the new vision. There was only "begrudging acceptance," even after cluster establishment, according to another lay leader. "Other clusters have voluntarily joined together," he noted, and "that would result in more shared vision, greater buy-in to the cluster." But he perceived the North Central Cluster as being forced by financial troubles to go forward without positive volition.

The Rev. Fred Valentine was a long-time servant of the churches in the area, in full- and part-time calls over the last four decades. A dedicated rural and small-church pastor, his was a trusted voice that helped to legitimate the cluster mission in its early stages. Valentine cast a shepherd's gaze upon the aches and pains of the people in the beginning of the cluster arrangements:

> It was the low point. Many [had] a defeatist attitude. You know: "We're really going to lose our local identification, our local involvement because we don't have a priest in the community." Probably [they were] even sensing that the church is going to be closed just because we can't maintain it that way. I think that was a very solid negative over the years in many of the congregations—particularly where they had [had] their priest.

Several recalled that "it was one priest, one church," as one woman said: "When I was little, we went to a village church, and the two closest [churches] would share a priest. That was much more comfortable" than the cluster, she said. Similarly, another woman declared:

> I don't like to deal with not having my own minister. I want the minister in my church to be *mine*. I don't want to have to wonder if I'm going to have this minister this week or that minister next week. And all of the ministers we have are good; it's not that. It's just that I want one minister and the continuity of that one minister continuously. That is my main problem. . . . I'm selfish, I guess.

Others insisted that the cluster and local church must conflict with one another, as if it were a zero-sum game for resources, new members, and current members' time. "This is *our* church. *Our* church. It's not the doorstep to the cluster church. It's *our* church. I have heard that over and over again," noted one layperson. But he added wryly that that attitude was "another part of the old wineskin that we're going to have to empty out. First of all," he argued, "it's not *your* church; it's God's church." In the second place, "if you want your church, you're going to have to give up something to somebody else so they can bring these four churches together." He concluded that "you have to change mindset, and that's very difficult to do."

Along with a change of mind comes a change of posture. Congregational members had been adjusting to shouldering the cluster "burden." As a lay staff member described it:

> So far, in my opinion the cluster hasn't improved [the burden on lay people]. We can't get people to serve on the cluster council, so the same people have been on the cluster council since I've been here. . . . Getting people to serve on the vestry is like pulling teeth.

For example, many parishioners spoke wearily of the "added burden" of cluster responsibilities heaped upon regular congregational duties. It is well known that small congregations exact an inordinate level of effort from a handful of committed leaders. With other resources scarce, small congregations often exploit the good-natured (and sometimes not-so-good-natured) willingness of some to keep things going through personal sacrifice of time, talents, and resources. As one person said in an interview, "You get a guilt complex because it's so small and there's no one else to do it."

Numerous interviews revealed aches and pains of congregational struggles continuing apace and sometimes exacerbated by cluster efforts. It may be that these data were the mark of slow adjustments to new congregational responsibilities and the breaking of codependence with the diocese, as Bishop Smith's book indicates. On the other hand, they may also be symptoms of inadequate preparation and relationship-building in cluster beginnings, as some interviews indicated. Some parishioners recognized, however, that the perceived "added burdens" were partly a function of retaining the autonomous power of congregational vestries, and a symptom of increasing lay power that was welcomed in other ways. Meanwhile, many parishioners did not indulge the temptation to blame diocese or bishop for their plight or their burdens. One woman stated:

> And our bishop that we have now had been extremely conscientious with working with us. I have never . . . seen another bishop as much as I have this one, and I've known a number of others. [He's] not just [working with] our cluster, but he holds regular Bible studies which you can go to.

The vision, leadership, and availability of the bishop had of course opened him to criticism, both reasonable and unreasonable. But the diocese was learning systematically as it pioneered in cluster ministries, and an important function of that was the bishop's willingness to work in partnership with people as they struggled with their local conditions.

The learning process had been as arduous for clergy as for laity. One parishioner spoke of the trying beginnings of the cluster:

> When we first started the cluster, I don't think the clergy had the right skill set. They too had been from the old model—one clergy, one congregation. And that's what their skills would allow them to do best. Whereas over time we got people who were committed to the cluster ministry, understood that, and accepted that.

While clergy might have been trained and bright enough to understand analytically the demographic and social challenges to which cluster ministry was a response, and they might have articulated the theology and practical vision of cooperative area mission, they still had many personal and professional adjustments to make. "This is a real challenge for any priest coming in," said one parishioner. She continued:

We've had extraordinary priests in the last ten to 12 years. I mean they could go anywhere, and they have, you know; the ones that left were picked for huge congregations in other places. Just wonderful people. But I don't know what they see in *this*, because this is a real challenge.

A vision of mission has guided clergy and laity through the challenges, as we will see below. But old patterns of behavior, on personal, professional and institutional levels, provided a constant hidden agenda of work to be done alongside the obvious, external work of clustering.

After the time of this study, the North Central Cluster experienced reorganization once again. St. Barnabas, in growing Bridgeport, entered a new arrangement with a neighboring congregation that shared the suburbanizing context on the Interstate 79 corridor. Grace, Transfiguration, and St. Matthias continued the North Central Cluster, including attention to Philippi in their area mission. The missioner moved his residence to Bridgeport from Buckhannon. The cluster mission could then build upon the shared context of county-seat towns—and small colleges in each except Grafton—without stretching to accommodate the very different mission context of Bridgeport and the congregational revitalization necessary for St. Barnabas.

Ministries

In a report from early 1998, Kelly Marshall identified an array of ministry activities that he deemed "what's working" in the North Central Cluster. Among them were the important but basic missional functions of congregations: weekly worship, pastoral care to members, opportunities for Christian education, maintaining facilities, and active vestries. In addition, the congregations participated in certain social-ministry activities at a local level. Insofar as the cluster built up basic congregational ministry, it has been secondarily responsible for these ministries. If one looked for that which occurred precisely because the cluster was in place, and probably wouldn't have occurred without it, there were four items: (1) Stimulating and supporting a local layperson moving into ordained ministry, (2) raising laypeople into pastoral-care roles, (3) widening the scope and power of lay leadership in local and diocesan affairs, and (4) sharing of lay talent and relationships between the congregations of the cluster. Interviews confirmed these latter areas noted by the missioner.

The North Central Cluster had a delightful individual named Fred Bird working toward becoming an ordained priest through a diocesan-based program. Labeled a "local canon priest" or "Canon 9 priest," after the ecclesiastical directive that structures it (see pages 57-58), the status is similar to "alternate routes" to ordained ministries in other denominations. Fred Bird, a member of Grace Church in Elkins, was already preaching and providing pastoral care throughout the cluster while he was studying in the diocesan training program.

Father Fred Valentine cited Fred Bird's "growing excitement" in ministry as a mark of the cluster raising indigenous and lay leadership. Bird himself attributed his journey toward ordination to the climate and needs of both the small church and the cluster. He compared the situation to what he imagined would be the case in a large congregation:

> If I were a member of a large church, with two or more ordained seminary-trained priests, I probably wouldn't have a hint of doing this. First of all, they wouldn't need me for one thing. . . . I like to be needed, whatever I do.

Furthermore, Bird observed, his migration from lay leadership to ordained status was a major stimulant for the development of additional lay leaders. He saw the cluster "lifting up people at all levels of ministry, not just the Canon 9." He thought he could be effective throughout the cluster in raising lay leaders because he could say,

> Folks, I'm just a Joe like you. I've not been to seminary; they've given me three years of some off-campus work, study on some things. I think that will help things.

"My view," said Bird, "is that there's at least two or three people in each church that we might somehow or other get them turned around and get the Spirit's calling." In that way, he thought, other laity would "pick up this idea and get going with it too." Several people throughout the cluster articulated the vision that some day there would be a Canon 9 priest from each of the cluster congregations, serving on a clergy team that would include at least two seminary-trained priests.

Lay pastoral visitors were trained and just beginning their work at the time of this study. Making hospital and home visits in their locale, the lay visitors were to supplement clergy visitation with active care among the laity. One pastoral visitor explained that at one time "we didn't really pray as easily" in public situations, "but now I realize the prayers I'm saying by myself can be used for somebody else." Once having contributed to the public ministry of the cluster, the lay pastoral visitors experienced benefits from their increased involvement, and brought benefits to the clergy who could accept it. Father Fred Valentine noted:

> It broadens them [through] that opportunity, you know, of a sense of ministry. We've always talked about the clergy are about 1 percent of the church and all the laity were 99, but you know the old-fashioned idea of the clergy operating the church and being the chief pastor and all. . . . I think it's unfortunate for clergy or ministers who get threatened by lay involvement or lay responsibility. 'Cause that has to be if it's going to be meaningful.

Father Valentine reflected on the new roles of lay pastoral visitors, but his observation applied to the overall expansion of lay power in the cluster.

With the assumption of wider lay power, there had necessarily been some growing pains on the way to the benefits. "We've had to assume much more of the ministry," one informed layperson said. "We do very well in the areas of education and pastoral ministry," she noted. "But I don't think we necessarily would have done so well if we hadn't been forced to do it," was her assessment. The professionals had tried to equip the laity for leadership, one woman noted. "However, they are meeting the resistance of West Virginians." She suggested that to rouse people to wider responsibilities, "you sort of coax it into them and make them think it's their idea." Others noticed lay power rising through the hard process of taking on the difficult tasks of church management and being forced to be responsible for themselves. "My perception," said one lay leader with experience in finances, "is that the cluster has forced us to be better organized, develop better budgets, to identify and clarify our mission, make us decide what we want to do, [and choose] a direction." For prompting those growth areas, he thought the cluster was "a very positive thing," even as he remained critical of key drawbacks.

On the positive side, increased lay power and responsibility were bolstered by the depth and breadth born of four congregations working together. "Taking on a project," observed a laywoman, "we don't have to see it through ourselves, just one little church. You have people power from the other churches. I think that gives you a little more security with taking on projects because you know there's help." Such cooperation must eventually expand the participants' vision of themselves and their ministries, Father Valentine said. In giving power to the laity, the cluster opened "the opportunity to develop a larger concept of what ministry and church life is in the day and age we're living in." Valentine continued:

> To come together to work on things and plan things and deal with one another in this manner will eventually strengthen the churches by helping them have a bigger vision of what's out there today and what needs to be if we're going to continue to function and survive.

Moreover, Valentine observed out of his long experience in ministry that people were "sensing that it's important, and they can get excited about it." Although "there are always those who talk about advantages and those who cite disadvantages or felt like they were threatened or going to lose something," Valentine said he thought that "in the last three years the trend has really been upward." Because "more of the leadership of the parish [was] functioning in key roles," they were in turn "more willing to think positively about what we should do," Valentine observed. Thus a wider breadth of lay power was born amid the growing pains of cluster formation.

Especially among those carrying the burdens of operation together, and secondarily among all cluster laity, fellowship and sharing of lay talent increased. While many noted that there was a long way to go on this front, a number of people celebrated the rewarding joint worship services. "The high points to me," reflected Fred Bird, "have been when we've done cooperative services":

> Those have really been meaningful. Everybody comes away from them saying, gosh, I didn't know it was gonna be like this. . . . I like small churches, but I like going to a big church sometimes just to hear the music, hear the singing with 200 voices . . . that's a highlight to me.

A related highlight, Bird continued, "is when we can pool resources and say, OK, we don't have this over here in Grafton, but we've got somebody we can call on over here in Bridgeport." As this exchange was taking place, a part-time staff member observed, "We're finding out that there are neat, interesting people in the cluster. . . . We're gaining an appreciation of the diversity of people." For some who had transplanted themselves into north-central West Virginia, the larger numbers of participants in activities and worship could be comforting. One leader who was nurtured in very large congregations noticed that in the smaller churches "there wasn't room for anybody to be disenchanted or upset with the priest, or how we operate, or the vestry. . . . You can't afford to lose a single person here." When the cluster came into being, he said:

> It was kind of nice; it kind of opened the doors. And now instead of one church you had four. And that was kind of nice because it gave you a chance to see more people, meet more people. For us, that was a real advantage.

The depth and breadth of a larger constituency gave a little political leeway in his view, besides providing more talent and being interesting socially. Sensitively, this leader noted that dealing with the larger group of people represented "a real loss" to those who clung to the intimacy and tight power structure of the smaller units, and "who don't want to go beyond that."

The vision was shifting from autonomous congregational ministries, managed by priests, to a cooperative area ministry enacted by a whole team of laity, shepherded by priests. Next we take a look at the way that the vision was taking root and developing in context.

Vision

The North Central Cluster was in the springtime of its development, and the vision of its people was emerging organically in context. Those most obser-vant of the cluster process recognized the struggle involved with learning new patterns of behavior, even while still depending on the strengths of traditions. The vision that was emerging from the people of the North Central Cluster was that planted by the bishop. Borrowing a New Testament image, many spoke of "new wineskins" taking the place of "old wineskins" to describe the structural changes and behavioral adjustments. While begin-ning to utter this vision as their own, the laity and staff of the cluster mingled expressions of the frustrations encountered along the way, the fear of the unknown, and the grief of leaving behind formerly comfortable choices. But overall, there was a noticeable shift in expectations and attitudes, at least on the part of some deeply engaged lay leaders and staff.

The possibility of pursuing a separate path from the cluster was not a realistic option for any of the four congregations at the time of this study. Independence as an idea had longevity well beyond its actual viability, however. One astute layperson noted:

> I imagine some people here would still like to have "their own priest," as they would say. Someone who would be only here and especially for them. I think many of us who have been on the vestry or been on the cluster council or worked with those groups— I don't think we'd ever want to go back to just our own little church. The mission is just too narrow and the focus is too inward. So I think one of the really positive aspects of cluster ministry is that you cannot think for very long just about yourself. You just are forced to look at something bigger than you are. And of course that is . . . frustrating! And I think it is still a difficult and frustrating thing for some of us.

Beyond the frustration was a new realm of positive spiritual growth for individuals and congregational communities, she contended. As individual communities became intimately aware of one another, there was not only the comfort of sharing the same plight but also the impetus to self-reflection. "When you see some of the ways someone else does it, then it can cause you to ask a couple of questions: Why are we doing this? What's the purpose of that?"

An important element of the emerging vision was acknowledgment of congregational traditions and identities. "When you are a cluster," said the layperson quoted above, "you realize that there are . . . other churches [that] hold their particular traditions just as dearly as you do. So it makes you step back a bit and think about the meaning and purpose of tradition." In turn, there was the benefit of growth through intense interaction, which she surmised was "an underlying belief in clusters: the interaction." On the other hand, the irony of avoiding interaction did not escape her. "I mean, you just can't sit there and hang on to a tradition *[laughs]*, or you're going to, you know, die, I think."

Beyond the benefits of institutional survival, there was the excitement of "maybe getting back to the original thoughts about the way the church is to spread," noted one man. "Maybe it will require a deeper sense of spirituality in all of us in order to continue," he mused. Others upheld the notion of lay ministry specifically at this point. "What you really want to see," said one man, "are lay pastoral visitors to visit people, and training, training, training for the laity so that we can get to the point that we could do this thing for ourselves." That, he said, is "how I envision this thing is supposed to work." And Fred Bird, the emerging Canon 9 priest, envisioned the fruition of the laity's ministry as the centerpiece of the new vision:

> Going back to that old model when the minister or the priest did everything for people, people didn't have to dig deep in themselves for some resources and skills and capabilities, whether it's visiting the sick or whatever. I think there's lots of people in the church if they were given the opportunity and some training on how to interview and be with people, they could be just as effective or even more effective than anybody else.

Such engagement and commitment were personally rewarding for a number of laity, and an integral part of their vision for the cluster. One leader spoke of being at a stage in life when recognizing legacy and assuring it is passed on is extremely important:

> I really feel that we inherited a legacy here. I'm now at an age where I have to be one of the people who makes sure that this stays open, that it works, and that there's something here for the children. I mean, it was here when I came along. And all of us now who are responsible for the growth, responsible for the finances, responsible for the building, responsible for the theology and everything that goes on, we have to have something to say about that. Be sure that it continues. It's our legacy now, and we've got to be sure that we pass on something that's as solid as when we inherited it.

In taking responsibility for the legacy, the laity were simultaneously taking responsibility for the church's mission itself. The cluster provided a context for true ownership and responsibility for that legacy, even while it demanded more effort of its lay and clergy leadership. Legacy and churches might continue without the "direction" that the cluster set, the man quoted above recognized, but the cluster gave something more: a vision. He thought that two of the congregations could have continued without the cluster, but that they would have done so

> with no vision. And I hate that. I want to see where I'm going, and I want to know when I get there and I want to say to someone this is what you're going to have to do . . . if it's going to be here in 2000 and 2005 and 2010.

The vision was taking root in context, gaining a momentum earned through the hard work and tears and tenacious commitment of Christians laboring day to day. At times those with the vision had been like voices in the wilderness, for the task was mighty and the challenges daunting. Yet there was strength of spirit and the intangible benefits of struggling for something worthwhile evident in the visionary perspectives of the lay leaders of the cluster. In their own way, they were becoming missionaries to their local communities, and the satisfactions of vibrant church mission were coming around the corner for them.

Tensions

Along with growing opportunities, tensions inevitably develop in communal and institutional life. In contrast to the growing pains that came with founding the cluster and shifting the mindset away from "one pastor for one church," the tensions arose from the cluster structure once it was up and running.

Geography was the most serious ongoing tension within the cluster. For the missioner, it was a daily cross to bear. One parishioner looked askance at the missioner's geographic challenge, and she remarked that to do the job "you'd have to be in love with your car." A related issue was less pastoral presence from a single central ordained figure. "I want my three-year-old to grow with a close rapport with the priest, not the pastoral visitor who's going to come and go," said a young mother. Her hope was "that there's this other figure in [the child's] life with which to grow, you know, just like a family doctor." Similarly, pastoral presence in each community was reduced by itineracy. "Down on that main street," said a Grafton woman, "very few people know who the Episcopal priest is when [the priests] come and go like this." With the main priest on the move, "there is jealousy for the priest," said another. Parishioners ask, "Why is he spending so much time with that other church?" The geographic and social tension surrounding the missioner would be alleviated by the addition of Canon 9 priests in each community, or by some geographic reconfiguration. Laity, too, stretched themselves over distances, as one parishioner observed. "It is not a close-knit cluster," he said. "It would be different," he said, "with two or three churches in adjoining towns."

Another tension pitted local initiative against wider governance. Some negotiation of power necessarily came from the overlapping of a central cluster and local vestries on the same turf. "Basically, the cluster council has to be the authority," said one lay leader. "But somehow you've got to give each one of the churches their individuality," he added, "to make them feel that their church is still a part of the community as opposed to a part of the geographic area." In turn, "the cluster council cannot do anything without the approval of the four vestries." On a larger scale, the individual vestries perhaps lost a sense of initiative and responsibility in light of the crucial role of the diocese and cluster council in oversight. Besides the danger of financial dependency upon the diocese, one leader noted, there was another significant problem:

> Vestries maybe aren't as strong as they were before, because they wait for the cluster to sort of give them direction and then they react. I saw a little change when I was on the vestry that maybe we didn't see our job as so vital as we did before. Because now we had a bigger committee, you know in the cluster you have [a] finance committee and everything and they were also looking out for the viability of the cluster. And if we couldn't give as much money to the cluster as we had, we sort of looked at that as a cluster problem rather than our church problem. Whereas before when we had to be self-sufficient, if we had a financial problem we had to resolve it.

The leader worried about a pattern of "laxity," of "you telling me you're going to do something and then you just don't do it because you know there's another group that might." That could be a problem up close between vestries and the cluster council; it could also be "the same weakness" in relation to the diocese. Thinking "we don't have to worry about the money because [the diocese is] there," causes local initiative to wane in the throes of a dependency syndrome. The irony is that the very structure created to eliminate dependency could actually foster it.

Finally, a significant tension in the life of the cluster was the continuing task of helping people adjust to change, particularly the change to cluster structure and governance. Father Valentine noted that the bishop, for example, gave "the kind of leadership necessary in providing the resources for cluster development." However, he continued:

> In some ways the bishop needs to be careful in the way he administers and develops the cluster. He's one of the leaders in developing cluster ministry . . . and he's enthusiastic. I feel sometimes in terms of sitting down with a group and discussing cluster and the possibilities and all, and stressing lay leadership and lay decision-making that sometimes in his role he gets too far ahead of the laity, or doesn't maybe give them enough preparation or time to assimilate what he's vitally interested in. Like a parish priest sometimes can go in and get way ahead.

The bishop's leadership was structurally removed from the everyday context of any parish. The missioner, however, was in a position to foster adaptation to change on a daily basis. One parishioner noticed Father Marshall doing this consistently with folk who were still having a hard time with clustering. He explained:

> He has several people who aren't sure the cluster is what they want. And he says, nobody is sure if the cluster really is what anybody wants. We have to wait and see. Let's work it and give it our full attention and see what happens. Maybe the way we're set up here is wrong. Maybe there's too much space. He doesn't come in and just say, "We've got a cluster; you've got to keep the cluster." He doesn't beat you over the head with it. And yet, I think he's convinced that that's about the only way we're all gonna continue, is to have some relationship.

Why It Works

The role of the missioner, and having an individual such as Father Kelly Marshall in that role, was a main reason why the North Central Cluster was working. "The missioner is the cluster," said one elder at Grafton. "He organizes the events," and "the priest is very important because we need a leader," he added. These comments in part reflected the longevity of the clergy-centered model of ministry in West Virginia, but they also disclosed the crucial role of the cluster leader in the new mission model.

A strategic element in the missioner's opportunity to embody the cooperative parish was his call to the entire cluster, distinct from a call to one or more individual congregations. Father Valentine explained:

> When Father Kelly came on, he came to the cluster and not particularly identified with any one congregation. [It was] a very positive thing. It gave us an opportunity to go into a new kind of relationship. No one congregation was in a sense able to identify or claim the missioner as their priest, which helped, I think, in the transition.

Furthermore, the ability to work with small congregations and not to be "too hung up on programs," was as important as the organizational and administrative skills for a large organization, a layperson added. The missioner united the parish under a balance of directive leadership and quiet understanding. "When Kelly came," noted one influential observer, "he said, 'You're going to do this, and you're going to do this,' and he stood them all on their heads." At the same time, the cluster worked because the missioner was "adaptable" and "a good listener," noted another person. A cluster director must proceed in such a fashion "because from each of these churches comes a different story," noted one. The key listener must understand and weave together the stories. This was happening in the North Central Cluster because of a dedicated and talented missioner.

The other side of why the cluster worked was the growing lay engagement and investment, embodying the cooperative ministry in tandem with the missioner. A sense of purpose, commitment, and enjoyment that sealed the cluster covenant was welling up among the lay leaders. One parishioner compared his cluster to other churches to evoke a sense of the not yet fully defined genius of the cooperative:

I've watched what's happening to the other churches. The other churches are all being forced to go the same route. And it's hard for me to believe it's strictly financial. Because almost every organization I know, even though things are tight, still limps along. And maybe as a credit to churches, we don't want to limp along, we want to be strong.

Another parishioner found it helpful to learn the problems that the other small churches have in common, because "it has probably driven us closer together" to know that strength is a costly affair in most phases of mission. Laypeople were discovering their own strength and their church's potential. Another lay leader summarized: "The cluster gives us some hope and some faith that things will get better. That we can rely on each other." Therefore, he thought that even "if we had a million bucks" and "could go out and buy, if you will, some new members," they'd stay with the cluster because of its emerging strength. The people were looking within themselves and their community of faith, and finding a sinewy strength that they previously didn't know they had.

Future

When parishioners and staff of the North Central Cluster looked to the future, their newness as an organization called forth a number of worries. Few concrete positive developments were articulated in interviews because the struggling cluster leaders had not yet emerged onto a plateau in their work from which they might see hopeful new horizons. The worries for the future readily surfaced, and not surprisingly they mirrored the aches and tensions cited above.

The biggest challenge, one leader thought, was "not to have a survival mentality." That would be difficult, since each congregation had declined in membership over the previous decade. One leader hoped, however, to solidify goals and "build a little more cohesiveness" around the chosen mission, to stem the trends. A grand reversal would be to become financially independent, he thought. Being supported by the diocese was "not unlike being on the public dole," said one official with experience in public institutions. "If you don't get off of it," he concluded, "it just becomes a way of life." The "flip side," he said, was that for the North Central Cluster "it may take the dedication of more [external] resources before it requires less or no resources" from without. Being in that precarious position, the young organization was not yet to a point of being able to develop and support "good leadership development or succession plans," noted another. He compared the cluster to his own business and other organizations, and observed:

> Succession planning, leadership training, and development usually occur within organizations that are already successful or [have] reached a point when they are successful.

Complete liberty from "survival mentality" would require the emergence of a web of self-supporting and self-perpetuating leadership.

In the short term, however, "sustained leadership" by the missioner "over a period of years" would hold the cluster together and continue to solidify it. Father Valentine cited the gifts that the missioner could give to the cluster: "vision, motivation, leadership, and good programming ideas." On a more important level, however, the missioner need not "be strong in all of those areas" but should "be flexible enough to work with other people and receive their input." Father Valentine saw this taking place in the ministry of Kelly Marshall, and he hoped it would continue throughout a much-needed period of stability.

The development of a team of Canon 9 priests and other staff would go a long way toward supporting the needed stability in the central missioner role. Geography continued to be a worry for the future articulated by many. A larger pastoral staff would mitigate the threat that geography posed to the integration of individual congregational ministries with overall cluster mission. The reconfiguration that took place after this study improved this worrisome frontier, but distance is still not to be underestimated as a problem in the reconfigured cluster.

For the few who could look up from the arduous work of beginning the North Central Cluster, the future did hold promise. One woman recommended that "You should take heart by small accomplishments rather than expecting that it's just going to happen." She cautioned, "You know, you're not going to get it all at once." With a further glance into the future, another parishioner spoke of where she would like the cluster to be in ten years. "I'd still like it to be in a cluster," she said. "I'd like us to grow, but I wouldn't want us to grow so that we could have our own priest." She suggested, "That would be a step backward." Instead of "regressing," she preferred that the Christians of the North Central Cluster would "grow spiritually."

CHAPTER 3

Upper Sand Mountain Parish, Alabama

Upper Sand Mtn. Parish

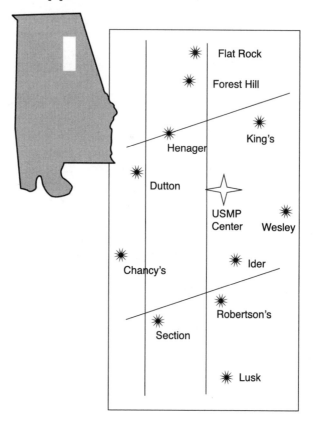

THE UPPER SAND MOUNTAIN PARISH

North Alabama Conference, United Methodist Church

Headquarters: Sylvania, Alabama

Executive Director: The Rev. Dorsey Walker

Cooperative makeup: 11 United Methodist congregations

Birthdate: 1969

Special Ministries: Gleaning Project, a cannery, Gardens of Plenty,
housing ministry, solar projects, clothing shop,
Christmas toy stores,emergency assistance, youth ministry,
mission trips to Russia

Staff: executive director, three ordained full-time ministers,
a part-time local minister, two certified lay speakers (bivocational),
youth staffer, "US-2" missionary, summer intern,
and parish secretary

USMP Council

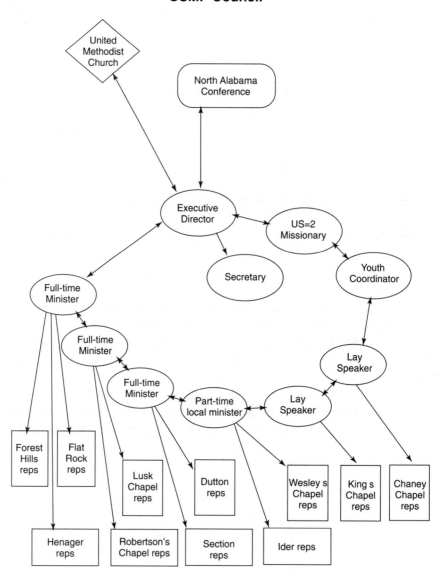

Upper Sand Mountain Parish, Alabama

T his parish saved my life," exclaimed a lay worker running the Better Way Shoppe. At a time when she, her husband, and children were in acute need, the Upper Sand Mountain Parish (USMP) in northern Alabama intervened not only with immediate emergency help but also with a longer-term plan to help them escape their economic and emotional crisis. She continues to count on the support of the parish as an emotional and physical safety net that keeps her and her husband living meaningful lives.

People like this family whose lives have been changed because of the ministry of USMP have kept the director and his wife enthusiastically involved in this ministry for 25 years and counting. Says the director, the Rev. Dorsey Walker:

> Brenda and I never imagined ourselves being in one place so long. We continue to be at USMP because of a strong sense of being where God wants us to be. This is affirmed for us by the ongoing good support of parish churches and community people. There is no doubt in our minds that God has brought this ministry into being for this particular time and place and that God continues to move among us to empower it by God's Spirit. We, therefore, are confident as we trust in God to lead us into the future.

Context

USMP is arguably the most well-known rural cooperative in the United Methodist Church. Its ministry originates from 11 small-membership congregations located in Dekalb and Jackson counties, at the northeast corner of Alabama. As we will see, the parish has a wide-ranging ministry that reaches as far as Russia and includes outside work groups from as far away as Pennsylvania and Texas. The headquarters of the parish, consisting of offices, the thrift store, a counseling center, a cannery, and storage, is in Sylvania, Alabama.

The parish serves more than 800 square miles on a long sandy plateau rising 1,400 feet above sea level. Natural and artificial boundaries border the study area: To the north is the Alabama-Tennessee border; to the east is Interstate 59 and the county seat, Fort Payne; to the south is state Highway 35, and to the west runs the mighty Tennessee River and the county seat, Scottsboro. When the authors visited the cooperative, we drove down Interstate 59 from Chattanooga, Tennessee, traveling along the valley forming the east boundary of Sand Mountain. You can ascend the mountain at many different points, but all roads up were a steep climb. Once on the mountain, we encountered a relatively flat plateau that may be from 60 to 70 miles long from north to south and 25 to 30 miles wide. When we went to the west side of the plateau, we again encountered a steep decline to the Tennessee River. The shopping malls, motels, and most jobs are off the mountains in the valleys to the east or west, especially in Fort Payne and Scottsboro. Some residents commute to jobs from the north end of Sand Mountain to Chattanooga or from the west side to Huntsville, Alabama. The commute to either city is more than an hour.

Located in the southern extremities of the Appalachian Mountain chain that extends from New York to Alabama, the region and people are characterized by much that identifies Appalachian mountain people. A history issued by the United Methodist church described Upper Sand Mountain succinctly:

> People suffer from the tremendous exploitation that has been imposed upon them and the region where they live. Natural resources—minerals, timber, coal, etc. have been stripped away by absentee investors who take profits and benefits outside of local communities and leave them impoverished. Local tax bases are not available to provide needed community services.[1]

The people have a strong streak of independence and self-reliance, of hope and pride, which continues to give them renewed determination.

Sand Mountain is one of the most densely populated agricultural area in the United States. Its economy is based on agriculture and small garment manufacturing, such as sock mills.[2] Because of the sandy soil, farmers could not grow large crops on the plateau until the 1950s, when commercial fertilizers came into common use. Today, farmers raise hogs and poultry and, to a lesser degree, grow cotton, hay, potatoes, and vegetables. Coal deposits in this area are minimal and have already been mined to levels that are no longer profitable to pursue. There are large stands of timber, many of which are difficult to reach. Many of the problems associated with mining and the lumber industries throughout the Appalachian region are found in the Sand Mountain area.

The mountain is considered an area of no significant growth. Population in the area is approximately 54,000, with a projected increase of 1,838 between 1995 and 2000—a 3.4 percent rise. The overall U.S. population is expected to increase 4.7 percent in the same time frame. From 1980 to 1990 this area experienced a 2.5 percent decrease. The average family size is 4.2; the average household has 2.58 people.[3]

Anglos represent 98 percent of the study area's population. Other racial groups make up 2 percent, well below the national average of 26 percent.[4] While there is almost no African-American presence on the mountain, the Ku Klux Klan is active there. Each summer from the latter part of June through the end of August, Spanish-speaking migrant workers of Mexican heritage come to the mountain to harvest potatoes and other produce. Emergency help, the food pantry, the thrift shop, and medical care enabled by USMP serve the migrant workers during these months. Open-air worship services in Spanish, children's programs, youth recreational activities and cookouts are also a part of the parish migrant ministry.

On Upper Sand Mountain, almost half of the population, 43.6 percent, does not have a high school education or GED (general equivalency diploma). Approximately 10 percent of the people have attended college and earned an associate degree or higher. In 1991, Dekalb County ranked last in Alabama for local funding of education. One encouraging sign: A two-year community college has been started recently on the mountain to enable local residents to attend college.

In the employment arena, white-collar workers compose roughly 15 percent of the work force. Most of these jobs are in management, sales, education, and administrative support. Blue-collar jobs and support services make up 85 percent of the work force. The per-capita income is a little over $13,000. Some 33 percent of the population lives below the poverty level for a family of four ($16,450). The median household income is $27,300.[5]

Given this income level, housing is expensive. The median cost of a home is $52,395, while rent averages $3,120 per year. Typically the rent does not include utilities, and normally the housing is a two-bedroom mobile home. Houses in the $120,000- $200,000 range are rare.[6] According to Dorsey Walker, director of Upper Sand Mountain Parish, it is hard "for a middle-income family to purchase a home, and the dream of buying a home for low-income families has vanished. As costs rise and credit becomes virtually impossible to acquire, owning a home becomes increasingly difficult."

The family structure is traditional, with 64 percent of the population married and 16.8 percent divorced or widowed. While commitment to marriage remains high compared to national statistics, almost 20 percent of the households report that domestic violence is a problem, and 22 percent report alcohol and drug abuse in the home.[7] One wonders whether the women in these relationships not only lack the support of the local culture to leave abusive relationships but also are without the resources to leave. In 1991, Alabama provided the lowest level of support for dependent children in the nation. Seventeen percent of Alabama's children under age 12 go hungry sometime each month. In 1986, Alabama's infant-mortality rate was the highest in the nation.[8]

Health care is an issue on Upper Sand Mountain. Rural health-care clinics provide medical care to area people, with fees on a sliding scale. Whereas the national average in 1991 was one physician for every 632 people, in Dekalb County the ratio is one physician for every 1,981 people, and in Jackson County one physician for every 2,448 people. People on Sand Mountain have a high incidence of diabetes. With limited resources, many families neglect preventive health care. There is also a high rate of teenage pregnancy.[9]

People in the study area are focused on personal spirituality and family. Their concerns listed in order from highest priority to lowest are: (1) a good church, (2) spiritual teachings, (3) dealing with drug and/or alcohol abuse, (4) adequate food, (5) teen/child problems, (6) divorce, (7) employment, and (8) child care.[10]

Approximately 88.5 percent of the population identify with the Christian tradition; 1.5 percent hold non-Christian beliefs, and 10 percent indicate no preference. However, 37.7 percent report that they are not involved with a congregation at this time. Those who report that they worship less than once a month increase the total of those not involved or marginally involved in the church to 52.7 percent.[11]

The largest denomination on Upper Sand Mountain is the Southern Baptist, comprising 40 percent of the respondents who claim a Christian tradition. The United Methodist Church claims 6.9 percent of the population. The remaining residents show a wide divergence of denominational preference. To understand the role of the church on Upper Sand Mountain, we need to remember that many Holiness and independent groups do not report their statistics. If we include these groups, then some studies suggest that the order of preference is: (1) Holiness churches, (2) Baptist, (3) Pentecostal, (4) Methodist, and (5) other. Snake-handling at religious services on Upper Sand Mountain has been well documented and still occurs regularly.[12] Another significant statistic is the almost total absence of liturgical denominations (Roman Catholic, Episcopal, Lutheran).[13]

Finally, "independence" and "local tribalism" are two of the strongest traits of these Appalachian people, not just today but from the time of the settlement of these people of primarily Scots/Irish roots. There is a sense of pride in self-reliance, and being a good neighbor sometimes means "minding one's own business and not bothering others." For example, stills that make "moonshine" continue to be common on the mountain. A church member offered to show us a still just a few miles from the church—but no one reports this illegal activity to law-enforcement authorities. According to a member of the Flat Rock congregation,

> The people of this area are strong, independent types. That is why they have been able to survive in bad times. They work hard, are honest, and will do what it takes to provide for their families. They have little and don't expect much in return. They survive because of determination.

Development

The Upper Sand Mountain Parish is a model for the United Methodist Church's national strategy for rural cooperative ministry. There are more than 1,500 United Methodist co-ops in the United States, but few of them do so many things, especially in serving the needs of the mountain people. Dorsey Walker came to two churches in the Upper Sand Mountain Parish in 1973, a year after graduation from seminary. By 1979, he was installed as the fourth director of the parish, working part-time while he continued as pastor of the two congregations. In 1984, he became full-time director of the parish. One church member remarked that "much of the scale of this success—most of it, some people will tell you—lies in the vision and the energy of . . . Dorsey Walker."[14] Like many of the people he serves, Walker grew up on a small family farm. His presence is part of every project. "Upper Sand Mountain is among the most creative rural cooperatives we have, especially in the Southeast," reports Gladys Campbell, executive secretary for town-and-country ministries of the denomination's General Board of Global Ministries.[15]

The parish was born in 1969 with two simple goals, according to Walker: "to strengthen local congregations in caring for their members and to provide opportunities for serving the needs of people in their communities and in the world beyond." Methodism had been a formative force in the early settlement of Upper Sand Mountain. However, most churches were unable to afford a full-time pastor and were placed in charges or circuits to share a pastor with other congregations. Some churches were served by part-time bivocational pastors. In a 1987 interview, Walker said, "These little churches were just dying." Some had fewer than 20 members. Area laypeople and ministers organized the cooperative with the help of the church's North Alabama Annual Conference, the General Board of Global Ministries, and Hinton Rural Life Center in Hayesville, North Carolina.[16]

Initially 17 churches worked to design a constitution for their ministry together. But when the constitution was completed in 1972, only 12 churches chose to ratify it and become charter members. Two churches withdrew in 1976, sensing the cooperative was not for them, leaving ten churches. There are now 11 churches in the cooperative, although not all the same churches as in 1976. One congregation has been disbanded; one dropped for lack of interest; two others joined or rejoined.[17]

The parish concept met some initial resistance: The concept was new, and it challenged congregations to expand their vision for shared ministry. Ownership has been a key issue across the years, especially as community projects develop. "Some in the congregations were suspicious that the parish might be an outside strategy to merge their churches into a few larger ones."[18] With Walker, the parish did two things that eased concerns regarding merger and assimilation: (1) Parish meetings and activities were rotated from church to church with all churches being equally acknowledged. The smallest, geographically most remote church hosts as many parish meetings and activities as any of the larger, more geographically central churches.

(2) The Parish Ministry Center was moved to Sylvania (a geographically central location) from Rainsville, where many small churches had suspected that the local congregation, Robertson's Chapel, had more control. Investment in parish ministries increased immensely through these two changes. Among the several congregations in the immediate area that have chosen not to join the parish is the largest United Methodist church on the mountain. The United Methodists claim almost 8,000 members in the two counties, whereas the combined membership in the Upper Sand Mountain Parish is 610.[19]

All the congregations in the parish are, and always have been, small. The largest, Robertson's Chapel, averages Sunday worship attendance between 60 and 70 people. Three—Section, Dutton, and Henager—involve 45 to 65 weekly. Four churches—Chaney's Chapel, Forest Hill, Wesley's Chapel, Lusk Chapel—have 20 to 30 in worship each Sunday, and two—Flat Rock and King's Chapel—count from 12 to15 in worship. Ider has an average worship attendance from five to eight. The parish combined weekly attendance is 450, and the average per congregation is 41.

Ministries

In the early 1980s, the parish started a *Gleaning Project*, based on the Old Testament concept of "gleaning," whereby a certain portion of crops was left unharvested in the fields for the benefit of widows, orphans, and strangers in the land. Parish members and local farmers were asked to donate extra vegetables for the parish pantry and canning program. The food was distributed to people in need on the mountain and beyond. Word of the project got around. According to Walker,

> Soon farmers were calling to donate truckloads of beans, cabbage, corn, potatoes, and peas. Vegetables that could not be marketed due to cosmetic blemishes, like cabbage with a little silt, or potatoes that wouldn't produce white chips. The first full truckload of 50,000 pounds of potatoes was donated by an area farmer after being refused in Orlando, Florida.

Walker contacted a minister friend in Birmingham, who contacted every social service agency she knew. He arranged with the farmer to haul the potatoes back to Birmingham, and the Gleaning Project grew from a local to a statewide project. Because the parish received so many potatoes during those early years, the Gleaning Project became one of the parish's most published activities. The parish works with Alabama's Job Training Placement Act Truck Drivers Program to ship vegetables to be shared through churches and nonprofit community organizations to families in need across Alabama. By 1986, for example, the governor's office asked the parish to coordinate the distribution of 150 tons of peas and okra from Draper Prison's farm.[20] Between 1984 and 1997, the parish recovered and shipped over 8 million pounds of fresh vegetables that would otherwise have been wasted. Until recent years, the availability of vegetable donations exceeded the money to harvest and package the food.[21]

When the parish was able to move to a full-time director in 1984, Walker had time to develop new avenues of service to the area and the state. The idea of a cannery, equipped to process the abundance of vegetables that were available, was born. To buy new equipment for a commercial cannery was too costly. Walker almost abandoned the idea until a local doctor gave the parish commercial appliances from a local restaurant. The *Better Way Cannery* was the result. The hope was that the cannery could employ low-income residents, along with using volunteers from mission service teams who come to the parish in July and August, to produce marketable products—canned vegetables, soup, and sauerkraut for urban soup kitchens and needy people across Alabama.

Gardens of Plenty is one of the earliest parish community ministries, begun in the 1970s. This ministry continues to provide seed and fertilizer for 450 to 500 families on low and fixed incomes to encourage vegetable gardening. Many participants are senior citizens with gardening skills but limited income for supplies. "For every dollar invested in this ministry, area families realize with their efforts [$50] in vegetables for their use and sharing with family and friends."[22] The parish also provides jars and lends canning equipment to encourage the preservation of food for better nutrition in the winter months for area people.

Throughout its history, the parish has established partnerships with youth volunteer service teams for the repair of area substandard housing. These projects are called *Heart and Hand Housing*. In 1986, Canterbury United Methodist Church in Birmingham initiated discussions about the possibility of raising money and recruiting skilled volunteers to build a complete house in a week's construction time. In summer 1987, more than 70 volunteers came "and with donations of $12,000 constructed the first passive solar, 960 square feet, three bedroom home in Sylvania for a family with three small children."[23] The Birmingham church pledged to raise funds, recruit volunteers, and construct one home each summer for ten years. In 1998, this church completed its 11th house. In 15 years, the parish has constructed 29 complete homes for families that otherwise would never have the opportunity for home ownership. The project provides interest-free rent-to-own loans to families and writes off labor costs over the repayment period. The families repay the cost of land and materials. Seventy-two children have moved into new homes with their families. According to Walker,

> There are many who think this is the best project the parish engages in to move families out of poverty. The project stabilizes families to become part of an ongoing community with children situated in one school system for their education.

Committed to good stewardship of resources and the environment, the parish initiated innovative *solar projects* in the 1970s. In 1984, the parish received a U.S. Department of Energy award for innovative solar projects. The parish worked with the local electrical cooperative, county councils on aging, and the high-school vocational agricultural classes to involve high-school vocational students (and their teachers) in leading workshops in which people build solar water heaters, hot-air panels, food dryers, and attached greenhouses. The project provided employment for teams of area youth and retired people. Since that time, over 350 solar projects have been constructed across the southeastern United States.

USMP runs the *Better Way Clothing Shoppe*. United Methodist churches and local community people donate clothing and small household items to the parish. Volunteers sort and size items for display and sales. Low-income women are hired to run the shop, which offers good-quality items at reasonable prices. For families in emergency situations or with special clothing needs, gift certificates are provided in the name of the parish church nearest to their place of residence. Profits are used for emergency aid to economically disadvantaged families.

Each Christmas the parish opens *Christmas toy stores* in four of the churches. Through donations, USMP provides new toys to the parents of from 250 to 300 children to support them in celebrating Christmas at home. Points are assigned to toys, with parents able to select items worth 20 to 25 points (equivalent to dollars) per child. A variety of stocking-stuffers and holiday foods are provided to the families.

The parish was instrumental in the development of *nutrition centers* for seniors on the mountain and managed a rural *transportation service* for ten to 12 years before County Councils on Aging were funded for these services. Walker told us, "A basic strategy of the parish has been to initiate services, help resource them and stabilize them with the goal of handing them off to others willing to operate and manage them."

The parish serves between 6,500 and 7,000 people each year with *emergency assistance*. Pastors in the cooperative commit one morning each week to counsel with clients at the ministry center. Emergency services provide food, medicines, and medical care, school supplies and workbooks, clothing, furniture, rent, and housing utilities. Over 40 percent of those served are children. The parish serves as a Local Recipient Organization for the mountain area of both counties in providing Federal Emergency Management Agency (FEMA) resources to families on the verge of becoming homeless.

The parish has always placed a premium on *youth ministry*, working with the youth in the area, as well as those in the churches. For over 20 years, the parish has conducted a weeklong summer program of *day camping* for area church and community children. Children prepare meals and enjoy games, stories, music, boating, fishing, crafts, worship, nature hikes, and an overnight campout.

More recently, the parish hired a coordinator for youth activities. The work has always been aimed not only at serving the youth in the parish but also at reaching community youth and children. After an area-wide survey of youth, the parish drew people from local churches, businesses, civic organizations, and schools to open the Sand Mountain Youth Center, "The Cage," in 1995. In 1997, the youth center hired a full-time coordinator and extended programs with a special focus on "at-risk" children and youth. In the spring of the following year, a tornado destroyed the youth center (no one was injured). The Rainsville American Legion responded by making its building available rent-free for a year to support the program. The youth center has a computer center online, an arts and crafts center, a big-screen television viewing area, a stage, a dance floor, pool tables, Ping Pong tables, air-hockey tables, and a jukebox. A multitude of activities are offered for area youth, including tutoring, GED classes, teen-pregnancy and drug-prevention programs, art classes, guitar classes, after-prom parties, and music—all to make the center a welcome hangout for youth.[24]

In cooperation with the Rural Chaplains Association and the support of the United Methodist General Board of Global Ministries, the parish organized a mission visit to rural Russia and Tajikistan (a former Soviet republic) in 1995. In 1996, USMP sponsored its first *mission/service trip* to Russia to make repairs in and around the Kromy orphanage. A service team has supported a rural Russian development project each year since. There has always been an intentional effort to include youth in these service teams. Since the first visit in 1995, the parish has envisioned the creation of a low-interest revolving loan fund to assist rural Russian communities, cooperatives and family farms in getting on their feet. The loan fund is being explored in partnership with the Orel Peace Foundation and the Rural Chaplains Association.

The parish has presented an Easter drama for three nights during Holy Week for 12 years. In addition to actors, numerous volunteers provide a drama choir, staging, lighting, makeup, publicity, and all the ingredients for a deeply moving re-enactment of the Last Supper. The offering from the drama has always provided support for "Partner Churches in Crisis" across the globe. In 1998 over $1,200 was raised for the Russian low-interest loan fund.[25]

Finally, USMP schedules regular *parishwide worship events and workshops* that rotate from church to church. There are "fifth Sunday night hymn-sings," lay-led revivals, Advent celebrations, mission festivals, Worldwide Communion Sunday observances, Ash Wednesday and Good Friday remembrances, children's Sabbath and Rural Life celebrations. Combined leadership training is provided for new church leaders, confirmation classes, lay speakers, vacation church school leaders, and children's workers. A parishwide praise band introduces innovative styles of worship and praise singing. As with all cooperatives, attendance at parishwide events is often not large. One pastor reports that events are attended by the host congregation and one or two people from the other parish churches. The issue, he says, is geographical—people don't want to travel 30 miles for an evening event.

Vision

In Dorsey Walker's modest and cramped office, every surface is piled high with "stuff"—books, magazines, papers, application forms, etc. It is an office in which only the occupant can find anything, and yet the "organized chaos" suggests something about the man. Walker, who is interested in almost everything, has an amazing ability to keep many different kinds of projects in his purview at one time.

Person after person whom we interviewed said that Walker is the heart and soul of USMP, and provides much of its vision. One layperson said, "Dorsey is the visionary. Everyone knows who he is. His gifts are love, hard work, and humility, as far as putting others' needs first." Members pointed to his vision, to his ability to "find" free or surplus foods or materials, and to his ability to get things done. According to the lay member, "Dorsey takes nothing, and makes something out of it." One pastor said of him, "Dorsey is an expert at raising funds. Dorsey is an expert at getting people to do things. He's always on the go, doing these things. He very seldom comes up short when there's a need for the parish." Another pastor said, "Because Dorsey has been here so long, he knows what it's like to run this parish, and it fits him like a glove. He has shaped it like he runs it, based on his feeling, habits, and convictions." Finally, a layperson expressed his views of Walker: "He can convince people to do just about anything. He alone has the creativity, personality, and ability to connect."

"The goal of it all," said Walker, "is to help rural families empower themselves."[26] On another occasion, Walker said, "Aside from giving a fish, so to speak, the parish provides resources for fishing, lessons in how to fish, and access to a place for fishing." Ending hunger, Walker argued, is a complex issue far beyond giving people food for the table. "It has to do with poverty, politics, distribution systems, waste habits of consumption, and indifference to the world out there."[27]

Thus, one part of the parish ministry is to provide immediate relief to people in need. A second is to teach them how better to provide for themselves. A third important aspect of the mission is to acquire resources from government, foundations, and community businesses that would not be as readily available to individual churches. With the reputation of the parish, and with Walker having been on the mountain for 25 years, the parish has become a powerful advocate for area families, churches, and communities. As one layperson put it, "Dorsey can be a thorn in the side of local government, because it's so difficult to get basic services on the mountain."

Another aspect of the ministry is critical to the parish's success. A diverse array of opportunities is available for members of the parish churches and community people to become involved in service projects on the mountain beyond their local congregations. From home-building, to transportation services, to receptionist duty, to the work of canning and stocking a food pantry, the parish makes service projects readily available to volunteers of all ages. This diversity attracts not only local residents but also volunteers from across the country and beyond.

Walker believes that the potential for ministry from small churches is greatest when the abundance of resources is pooled. The cooperative challenges people to increase their personal involvement not just in churches but in the community at large. Under his leadership, the parish contracts with individuals to do volunteer services, such as training women in nontraditional job skills. The parish continually asks, "How do we engage laypeople to serve?" Dorsey Walker describes it this way:

> It's coordinating life discovery. If you just leave people on their own initially, they don't really become connected very well. But if you say, "All right, we're going to do this together," and you're willing to help identify the resources, it enables the connections to be made. Such intention and purpose is felt on a local, national, and even global level.

Walker sees parish leaders and himself identifying projects or help needed, and his job is to find the resources—human, material, and monetary—to enable this ministry to happen.

In finding and obtaining resources, Walker has no peer. Alethea Tanner, the parish secretary, says fondly of Walker, "Dorsey can make you volunteer without you knowing it." One of the pastors in the cooperative described views of Walker as administrator.

> Some clergy and laity view him as the administrator up there [at the Parish Center]; others see him as one to work with. His personality is the key to his working style. In the staff covenants, each pastor pledges to give six hours a week to the parish. Dorsey invites them to volunteer additional time according to their unique gifts and inclinations. Some of the pastors follow through with the contract, some spend almost all of their energies on the co-op, and others spend almost all their time in the local congregations.

Not only is Walker adept at raising human resources, but also he is skilled at raising funds from outside the parish in wealthier suburban congregations and individuals, and in the wider United Methodist Church. He seeks donations of materials from companies and from farmers who have a surplus. In fact, the parish maintains a wide support network of people and companies that think of it first when they have something extra to give away. Walker is a master at making productive use of what the parish is given.

Walker attributes much of his approach to the influence of his father:

> He taught us children to learn to do with what we had. There wasn't a thing on earth he wasn't interested in. He used to say, "If there's something you need to know or are interested in, just go to the person that has the knowledge and ask them. Most are more than willing to help, especially old-timers." My biggest task is resourcing the project, raising support. Today the parish has a broad base of financial support that includes 150 to 200 contributors yearly.

Walker is similar to the other directors or leaders of church cooperatives. There is with him, as with almost all the others, the question of a democratic versus an authoritarian style of leadership. He is simply the hub around which the service ministry thrives. According to one layperson, "Dorsey's the key. A lot of people on the mountain would go hungry if it weren't for Dorsey. Most ideas come from Dorsey." Everyone agrees that Walker is a strong leader. He has high expectations of clergy and laity in USMP. Says one staff member: "Dorsey has high expectations but doesn't expect anything that he isn't willing to do himself. He can be a controller, telling you what to do and how to do it. As director, his sense of responsibility drives him to get things done his way, to move the people in a certain direction." This staff person greatly appreciates Walker's leadership but does say, "He's energetic. If he can do it, everyone else should be able to do it too. Not everybody can."

Walker says that the position of administrator of USMP may not even require an ordained minister; a skilled layperson could do the job. Which isn't to say that Walker doesn't view his position as the essence of ministry. He notes that he has been in the parish almost 25 years, since his first year out of seminary. From the beginning he and his wife, Brenda, chief volunteer of the parish, have been committed to challenging and securing resources for congregations to do more in caring for the communities around them than most have been prone to do. He puts his work in terms of vocation and notes that "what makes a leader is that God is calling them into the job. It is vocational work for both clergy and laity. It's great when you can do what you love to do and get paid for it!"

Finally, several people told us that you cannot talk about Dorsey Walker's vision without realizing that it is Dorsey's and Brenda's vision. This is a team ministry of husband and wife. One lay person said, "Brenda is Dorsey's 'rock of ages.' He does the footwork; she does the work. Brenda does a lot of manual labor in the parish center." Another layperson said, "Dorsey is irreplaceable, like the [Energizer] Bunny 'still going.' His wife is the same way. He gets the money, but she does the work."

Officially (although voluntarily), Brenda Walker is the coordinator of the Better Way Clothing Shoppe. She manages the many volunteers who sort, price, and size the merchandise that is given to USMP by community residents and United Methodist churches across north Alabama. She keeps a garden at home and arranges flowers for the churches. One pastor commented that she should be a horticulturist. Said another pastor: "Dorsey has a saint for a wife, a multitalented, wonderful woman that supports him 100 percent. And if she did not take care of everything on the home plate, Dorsey would not be able to do what he does. She and Dorsey are a team."

Dorsey Walker is not the only leader with a vision for USMP. The staff have their own way of stating the vision. In addition to the director, ministry staff is made up of three ordained full-time ministers appointed to serve two or three churches within the cooperative, a part-time local pastor serving two churches, and two certified lay speakers (bivocational). Of the full-time pastors, one spends as much time and energy as he can working for the wider parish. A second is extremely supportive of the parish and spends, according to his own estimate, approximately 20 percent of his time on parish matters. The third puts in his required six hours a week and is generally supportive of the parish, but complains that the parish makes too many demands on individual pastors, whose primary calling is to local churches.

The Rev. Donald Barnett, one of the full-time ministers, now in his ninth year of service in USMP, at one time served six local churches and was a part-time rural chaplain on the parish staff. Now he serves three churches. One of his responsibilities is training lay speakers. He credits the parish with enabling him to thrive in this setting and to stay so long, with such enthusiasm for and commitment to the ministry. Barnett has provided a concise listing of his vision of the main benefits of this cooperative.

1. The parish provides missional opportunities for members of the congregations. The cooperative allows them to provide services to the needy on the mountain that no single church could furnish by itself. For

example, the parish raised concerns about the lack of health facilities on the mountain. Primary health-care centers were built in Section and Flat Rock because the parish provided opportunities for community people to identify the need and provide for the health services. The primary health centers have sliding-scale fees that make these services available to all community residents regardless of ability to pay.

2. The cooperative brings people together from similar churches and communities across the mountain. "The folk are clannish, and people often don't know neighbors five miles away. The opportunity is for church members across the mountain to gather to do local outreach."

3. The parish gathers most of the resources for this outreach.

4. Few if any of these small churches would have full-time ministers without the cooperative but would be supplied by certified licensed lay speakers or be closed.

5. USMP provides leadership training for laity at the local level.

6. Having Walker as full-time director provides coordination and oversight of the entire operation, and time for promoting the cooperative.

7. USMP is able to provide resources to develop and help maintain work with youth on the mountain.

8. The parish provides weekly bulletins, copy machines, and computers. It also helps with church upkeep (roofs, painting, etc.).

9. The cooperative can pitch in and help a church with a major project. For example, one congregation is located toward the north end of Sand Mountain, where homes are being built for a coming influx of people who work in Chattanooga, Tennessee. This church decided to build a community center to increase outreach.

10. The parish identifies mission-partner churches and works to recruit volunteers to construct the building at half the normal cost.

The Rev. Ralph Johnson, a second full-time minister in USMP, served a charge within USMP, left to serve a charge outside the parish, and now has returned to serve different congregations in USMP. He states his vision of the parish and how it enhances ministry within the churches: "There's a theological reason for this enhancement. The parish gives me and my congregations the opportunity to get out from behind four walls in order to practice Christianity, to serve fellow human beings." He likens what occurs in Matt. 25:31-46, the Judgment of the Gentiles, where Jesus talks about serving the hungry, naked, and thirsty, as serving Christ. Johnson, who is an active participant in Confederate Civil War re-enactments, says:

> Excuse the military analogy, but it puts me in the trenches. It puts me in touch with real life. It gives me new fresh ways to think theologically, philosophically. Sometimes it's depressing and other times it's aggravating, but it gets me out from behind the pulpit.

"Mission co-op" is the phrase Johnson uses to describe USMP. Its main strength, he asserts, is the opportunity to serve. One of his fellow staff people says that Johnson is the kind of pastor who really fits into USMP because "Ralph Johnson, with a servant heart, likes the parish as a base of support for outreach." Johnson himself says that being part of a co-op makes him want to stay longer in his appointment.

The Rev. Les Brown, the third full-time minister in USMP, has been a part of the cooperative for a shorter period, three years. His wife, who works full time in a law office, is a stated supply pastor at another USMP congregation. Brown says that as long as these Christian churches are alive, the parish will be alive. "The 11 churches are like a family that only gets together for a funeral. When there is a need, they will be there for each other. Neither famine nor federal-funds stoppage will kill the parish." He describes the impact of serving at the parish center:

> It ought to be a requirement for each pastor to spend 90 days in a parish setting like this. Until you're willing to do this and accept it, you're not really understanding what Jesus is all about, I don't think. Until you're living in "taters" with people who stink, you don't understand charitable work. Many people live on survival level. All seminary grads ought to serve in small parishes like these.

Les Brown suggests that often it happens like this: "Local churches introduce the poor to the parish center, where real help can be offered. . . . Food and clothes are handed out on an as-needed basis. Medical care is provided for migrant workers and others. The parish center gives migrant workers and others in need what they require as a basis of support to establish living conditions. The parish center, to me, is the whole mountain."

In addition to the clergy, the paid staff includes a youth coordinator; a United Methodist US-2 missionary, assigned through the United Methodist General Board of Global Ministries; a summer intern; a part-time parish secretary; and a treasurer. The US-2 missionary is a young-adult volunteer, just out of college, committed to serving two years in service ministries somewhere in the United States while seeking to discern God's call to Christian service. According to Walker, many US-2 workers choose to enter the ordained ministry or full-time missionary service after completing the US-2 program. Summer interns, who have completed at least a year in college, spend June, July, and August in the cooperative. All these people have a share of the vision.

One part-time certified lay speaker said, "As far as the parish goes, it's done more good in this area to help people, and it's amazing that there's so many people in the area that still don't have a clue that it's here. The needy people know about it. Other local charges are slowly learning about it." Before the parish, there was no real outreach by the churches to the needy, as he recalls. No other denomination locally has a food pantry. Their attitude seems to be "We'll not give you nothing unless we can preach to you. We'll starve you down enough, then you'll hear about Jesus, then we'll feed you."

This lay speaker thinks that the food pantry and housing ministries are the most important aspects of USMP. "There's a lot of hungry people in this area," he said, adding, "Folks that have plenty find it difficult to believe that people are actually hungry. They say that hunger is mismanagement. But if they're hungry, they're hungry. USMP feeds a lot of people; many are children. You know by looking at them that they need help." Needless to say, this lay speaker, like all the others, works to keep his small congregation in the parish.

Dorsey Walker also empowers the staff for their ministry. For example, Debbie Taylor, the youth director, describes her experience in coming on the staff of USMP. "Upper Sand Mountain Parish gave me a starting point, a base of support within which I could do what I wanted to do to help people, especially kids. There are so many opportunities [to help people]. With a coordinator like Dorsey heading it up, it frees the staff to do the work they want to do."

Finally, lay volunteers capture the vision of USMP. One layperson said, "The parish provides a time and place for meaningful volunteerism." Another said the unique feature of the parish is "all the ministries we have, the different people we serve, programs we have. It's unique that these small-membership churches can do these things." Another layperson said, "For some people, the parish has expanded their notion of what it means to be the church. Without the parish we could survive as churches, but as for helping the needy, we would be very handicapped."

Tensions

We have already discovered that both great promise and unresolved (and often unresolvable) tensions occur in any cooperative. This cooperative is no exception.

1. Pastors and Staff

Don Barnett says that one of the inevitable tensions in any cooperative is the balance of time committed to the local congregations versus the parish as a whole. "Being a pastor here does take more time and commitment. One may spend too much time in parish volunteer work." However, he continues, "there is already this tension within a multiple-church charge. A charge with numerous churches places demands on schedule balance, evangelism efforts, and visitation time. A cooperative simply puts the need for cooperation on a larger scale."

When Ralph Johnson was asked if he put his priority on the congregations or on the wider parish, he said, "I probably lean toward the local congregations because of the daily interaction and the fact that the congregation pays my salary. The split is probably 80 percent congregations and 20 percent co-op, but there is not much tension between loyalty to the congregation or to the co-op."

While supportive of the parish, Les Brown experiences acutely the tension between his call to the local congregations under his charge and the responsibilities of the larger parish. First of all, there are many parish meetings. The staff meets twice a month, once quarterly for a pre-council and later quarterly for a council/commission meeting. In addition, pastors commit a morning a week to provide counseling at the parish center, with the expectation that they will volunteer additional time for other programs. For Brown, it creates problems for scheduling a regular day off:

> Dorsey relies too much on the pastors to put their churches aside at some point and take more of a role in the parish setting when really it is not necessary. . . . The capable staff at the parish center should provide the physical labor, while the local churches provide financial support. The local churches are demanding by themselves.

Debbie Taylor, the youth coordinator, articulated one source of possible tension.

> Part of the friction is that somehow you have to get the churches to see this as their ministry. . . . The problem comes when they [local congregations] don't see it as their church ministry, but as another thing that the parish wants them to do. Tension comes when the local churches view the parish as a separate entity.

In the history of USMP, a recurring issue has been consultation by the United Methodist bishop and district superintendent, with the parish director on the appointment of new pastors to parish churches. Some of those appointed in the past have been "lone rangers" who tended to work by themselves and did not support the cooperative personally or in their congregations.[28] As one longtime staff person put it, "We've had a few [pastors] that didn't want to cooperate, work well with others. It may be a drawback that a lot of Methodist ministers are not suited for team ministry." One of the pastors said there have been past issues with district superintendents who were supposed to consult with the parish director before assigning a pastor, but did not. This pastor thinks that the Methodist authority system tends to treat the parish like a neglected stepchild.

However, the pastors and staff agree that they are now part of a good pastoral staff, made up of people who are parish-minded and who value teamwork. They see the present bishop and district superintendent to be deliberate in consultation. In fact, most of the staff, including pastors, indicated that the cooperative encourages and provides them with resources for ministry and that they want to stay longer in their appointments. One pastor says, "At first, it's a call to local congregations, but then some of us really embrace cooperative ministry, really feel a part of it, enjoy it." One staff person said:

Those leaving seminary in search of big church, big bucks, forget why they're in ministry. Those who work in parish cooperative ministry get back to the reason why they went into ministry. The pay's not good, but the benefits are not in a dollar sense anyway.

A lay speaker said, "Most seminarians see [the] small parish as a means to an end—to move up the pay scale after paying their dues. But ministry isn't about salary and parsonages, but the experience of service."

2. Resistance

Internal. As a living, dynamic organism, USMP does live with tensions. One prominent issue is resistance to belonging to the parish, from both inside and outside the cooperative. While a clear majority of members in the parish churches support the cooperative, there is great variation in how involved the various churches are. One full- time minister, for example, told us that one of his congregations nearly pulled out of the cooperative, whereas the other church has many volunteers involved in the parish ministry.

What are the chief complaints among laity in USMP who resist the parish? First, as one of the pastors put it, "There is a psychological weakness that the parish is going to take over and parishioners will lose local congregational autonomy and identity." His comment: "We make a religion out of the preservation of our buildings and congregations." Maintaining local autonomy is the most important goal for some parishioners, and they want to limit the power of the parish over their congregation. Thus they are content to keep a division between local worship and spiritual life, on the one hand, and parish/social ministry, on the other. Concluded another pastor: "Parish, then, is viewed as a resource for the local churches, not an end in itself."

Second, as parish secretary Alethea Tanner expressed it, "There are people totally against it [USMP], because they think it takes focus away from local-church needs and focuses too heavily on a community of lazy, undeserving people." A pastor said of the resisters, "They think that you just shouldn't give something for nothing. They see a negative work ethic [on the part of the people helped], while they've seen hard times and worked through it alone. There is some resentment toward helping others when they believe no one offered to help them in their time of need." A layperson said, "A minority [of members of the USMP] are stubbornly anti-co-op. They believe that belonging to the co-op spreads the pastors too thin, detracting from local-church needs."

Moreover, one pastor points out that individuals, not whole congregations, are committed to the parish. "There are individuals, not whole churches on this mountain, who have bought into the parish." The picture, then, is one of committed individuals, many from some congregations and few from others, who are actively involved in parish volunteer work.

USMP never has every church represented at the council commission meetings. This passivity toward the parish organization has been variously explained. One lay speaker put it this way: "The majority of people don't want to take the time to ratify decisions. It's an extra meeting. The locals put trust in pastors, lay reps to council, and Dorsey [Walker]. Things work out well that way." A pastor talked about people being overworked. "The staff are doing more than the laity, who are ready to do hands-on work, but not planning/decision-making." Others suggested that at least 75 percent of the ideas come from the staff, who bring proposals to the commission for endorsement. If decisions are made that directly affect local congregations, they are brought back to local boards. Otherwise, parish decisions are made by the council, composed of five representatives from each parish church. However, there is rarely a problem with parish decisions needing local ratification. In short, the lay leadership of the congregations that make up USMP is content with the decisions the staff and a small core of church representatives make on their behalf. As one pastor put it, "People here are willing to let leaders make decisions." The staff, not surprisingly, would like to have more lay input.

External. Several small-membership United Methodist churches on Upper Sand Mountain choose not to belong to USMP. Their reasons for not belonging are similar to the reasons resisters within the parish give for their opposition. One notable United Methodist congregation that has never joined USMP and has no intention of doing so is Trinity Church, Sylvania. While the Parish Ministry Center is in Sylvania, none of the 11 parish churches is. Trinity is not only located close to the Parish Ministry Center; it is the largest United Methodist church on the mountain, with an average weekly attendance of 125 to 150 people and growing (from 106 members in 1969 to 263 members in 1998).

It is not surprising that Trinity chose not to belong to the cooperative. Many larger churches do not want any part of cooperative ministry. Often, larger churches think they can support the level of ministry they choose independently from other community churches. Furthermore, in Trinity's case, several people suggested that it is more attuned to Holiness and Baptist styles of worship and congregational life, while USMP churches are more traditionally Methodist in polity and liturgy.

Some churches on the mountain that are not United Methodist support USMP. One Baptist church, for example, gives $50 a month to USMP to support human-service ministries. From the beginning USMP has sought ways to make its ministry more ecumenical. According to Walker,

> Holiness and Baptist churches are present and work great as informal partners but are quite unwilling to become a 'structured' part of the cooperative. While USMP is a United Methodist co-op, its ministries would be greatly diminished without the support of area Holiness and Baptist churches.[29]

Walker explains his way of dealing with UMC congregations that choose not to become a formal part of UMSP:

> The co-op has cordial relations with all of the Methodist parishes in the area, though some wish to remain independent. A part of being a portion of the body is [that] the stronger is available to the weaker and, if they join together, then they aren't in competition. Rather than struggle just to pay a preacher and maintain a building, they can join together as one body and actually serve the community.

Walker wishes these churches were part of USMP but he is both unwilling and unable to force the issue.

Why It Works

Without a doubt the parish helps congregational members grow spiritually. They have a sense of belonging to the larger church as they reach out locally and globally. Their participation in ministries that have gained national recognition re-enacts the work of the Gospel in a social context. Together, the congregations continue to provide benevolence resources, not only through the parish, but also to the United Methodist Church as a whole.

Furthermore, the ability of the parish to focus and meet specific needs on the mountain is awe-inspiring to see. From parish day camps and youth centers, from Gardens of Plenty and solar housing, from the food pantry and thrift store, to help for people seeking employment—a service that has enabled many families to move toward self-sufficiency—this cooperative is phenomenal.

USMP works because of the vision, hard work, and ability to obtain resources on the part of Dorsey Walker. Alethea Tanner describes him as "energetic, creative, and resourceful." Walker empowers people. For example, he asked one of the members to run the cannery with no experience in canning. Walker said, "We'll learn together." According to that member, "So I did and ran the cannery for six weeks." However, beyond his ability to empower and enlist volunteers, beyond his amazing capacity to find resources, is Walker's basic attitude toward people in need. As one lay volunteer expressed it, "His gifts and talents are in ministering to the people. He doesn't judge. If people have a need, we're here to meet it. Dorsey is big on caring." His vision of care has "infected" both staff and lay volunteers, including the one who expressed her philosophy about helping out poor people: "In order to help the needy, you're going to help the greedy. To help those in dire need, you have to deal with everyone who comes in."

At the heart of USMP's mission is a biblical vision of the servant church—a modern-day attempt to address Matt. 25:31-46 by feeding the hungry, providing drink for the thirsty, supplying clothing for the naked, healing the sick, giving hospitality to the stranger (the migrant workers). But the parish secretary suggests a more intangible glue. When asked to describe the heart and center of USMP, she responded, "It's probably the caring, the love, the fellowship we have together. It's like a family—including staff and those whom we serve in the community each week. It becomes a relationship that you miss when you're not here; you get attached to these people." For her, the motivation of relationship and the love for the Lord ("without it a lot would be in vain") are the sources of USMP's strength.

Future

When asked about the future of USMP, one staff person said she wanted to see outreach bring growth to the local churches.

USMP does things without taking advantage of evangelistic opportunities. You can do things in the name of Christ without mentioning the name of Christ, and people don't come to the churches. Feeding people has not become an evangelistic message that turns people toward the churches.

USMP, in her opinion, needs to look for some kind of spiritual result, so that the people will know why they are being helped. A pastor said that while USMP provides meaningful opportunities to serve, people do not connect this service with helping their own congregation in any way. "If they're seeing the cooperative bringing people into the congregation, and the local congregation is growing in number from the cooperative, there would all of a sudden be a turn-around of being on board [i.e., belonging to USMP], I believe."

Thus, one concern for the future expressed by staff and laity in USMP is the need for focused *evangelism* efforts so that the parishes will be strong for ministry in the 21st century. One pastor said, "There must be a move toward expansion of evangelism efforts. There is a serious situation in the loss of local church membership. Traditional worship styles are losing whole generations of folk."

A related concern for the future is *lay involvement.* The US-2 worker, Jay Godfrey, said that staff and involved laity can be overworked. Only Godfrey and the director are full-time parish staff, and such lean staffing can lead to problems with lay/staff burnout. More volunteers are needed. A core of dedicated, caring people, especially retirees, serve as volunteers, and USMP counts on these people all the time. The parish needs to find ways to get other people involved.

Staff and lay leaders are concerned about the possible future loss of volunteers to run USMP's programs. One layperson said, "The main threat to the parish is a generational gap between the stalwart members who are aged and the younger members who are not active. When the older members die or leave, membership will drop. We need to build up the youth and Sunday school programming." Another lay member said, "The only visible threat is that without volunteers, the parish would die. We need young people, but most leave the mountain for a career. The big families that started the churches have died or left the mountain." A third layperson said simply, "There aren't enough young people. As older people go out from volunteer positions, there are questions as to who will replace them. Some of the most faithful members are getting on in years. The parish needs to pick up some younger people."

Thus, a relevant question for the future of USMP is, "Are there ways the parish can better focus on the need to evangelize, without compromising its social mission?" While we, the authors, agree that USMP would benefit by an emphasis on evangelism, we also want to point out what USMP has accomplished during its 30 years of existence. In an era when mainline churches have been losing members and when small-membership congregations have been most challenged to maintain membership, the parish has increased membership slightly. Overall, USMP's churches have increased in membership from 597 in 1969 to 610 today. During the same period, the United Methodist Church as a whole has experienced a 20 percent reduction in membership.

Does membership in USMP help these small congregations in the "at-risk" category maintain their own membership level rather than dissolve? The authors think so. Few, if any, of these congregations would grow more if they were on their own. In fact, the parish secretary said two United Methodist churches in the area she knows "are not involved in the parish and they're not growing—they're just sitting there; no volunteers, no outreach. Without the parish, mission is not a priority of identity or a way of understanding church." Let us underscore the importance of this last statement. For many members in the parish, USMP's mission is a way of identity and a way of understanding church. Thus, few members of USMP think the local churches are suffering numerically because they are involved in social outreach. In fact, USMP keeps some of these churches alive because it gives them a mission focus. Two or three of the parish congregations are growing significantly. Nor are all USMP congregations full of elderly people. Dutton Church, for example, is running about 65 people per Sunday with 25 to 30 children.

In a quiet, nonconfrontational way, USMP would like to expand its ministry into areas where, to date, it has had little impact. It has had little success in cracking the strong social characteristic of independence and clannishness at a level that would make possible dealing with issues of domestic violence, sexual abuse, drugs, and alcohol. With all of his insights, resources, and persuasive ability, Walker admits that the issue of abuse is hard to deal with. In his words,

Racism continues to be a concern as an increasing number of people of color move into what has been an almost exclusive Anglo population. The breakdown of families, with increases in teenage pregnancy and out-of-wedlock births, is a matter of concern. The combined social and economic crisis in agriculture and rural family business poses a never-ending challenge as the parish moves [into] the new millennium.

Walker would like to link surrounding communities together in an effort to be more inclusive in regard to both race and help for the economically disadvantaged.

Meanwhile, the vision of USMP continues to develop. USMP had applied for the assignment of a second US-2 missionary to begin service in September 1999. For that position, they requested priority for a Spanish-speaking person to relate to the increasing number of migrant workers who initially came into the area during the summer but now are staying year-round.

Above all, among the staff and lay leaders of USMP is a confidence that God has called them to this mission and will sustain it as they covenant together for the future. Again, while most mention the leaving of Dorsey Walker or his eventual retirement as a possible threat, they are convinced that a person of ability equal to Walker's, although different from him in many respects, will be appointed. In the end, their confidence for the future of USMP is, as Alethea Tanner said, "based in God's goodness and grace that has led them this far and will continue to lead them on."

CHAPTER 4

Milwaukee Strategy, Wisconsin

MILWAUKEE STRATEGY

Greater Milwaukee Synod,
Evangelical Lutheran Church in America

Headquarters: Milwaukee, Wisconsin

Coordinator: The Rev. Richard G. Deines

Cooperative makeup: 25 Milwaukee congregations,
two congregations in bordering suburbs, two campus ministries
(Marquette University and University of Wisconsin-Milwaukee),
SeedFolks Youth Ministry and Abundant Life Ministry

Birthdate: January 1, 1988 (with roots back to 1973)

Special Ministries: SeedFolks Youth Ministry (SIMBA, CHOICES,
Raising Our Sons and Daughters, Message in the Music,
Putting Down Stones, Summer Youth Work Programs),
Milwaukee Outreach Training Network (Vision Team,
Outreach Cadre, Neighborhood Ministers, Parish Nurse Program,
Mission Exploration Team, Mutual Mentoring for Pastors,
and Abundant Life Ministry), Lay School for Responsible Living,
and MICAH

Staff: Coordinator (Assistant to the bishop of the Greater
Milwaukee Synod for coalition development),
director of Abundant Life Ministry, director of SeedFolks Youth
Ministry, synod resource development director,
and half-time grant writer for Abundant Life Ministry

31 Coalition Ministries

(25 congregations in Milwaukee, two in bordering suburbs, two campus ministries (Marquette University and University of Wisconsin—Milwaukee campus), SeedFolks Youth Ministry and Abundant Life Ministry. Congregations are divided into six strategy areas.*

ELCA

Synod Bishop

Assistant to Bishop for Coalition Ministry

South:
Immanuel Faith
Ascension
(worships in three languages:
English, Hmong and Spanish)
Redeemer
Great Spirit
(Native American congregation)
Unity

North:
Cross,
Reformation
Hephatha
All Peoples
Incarnation
Abundant Life
Ministry

Far North:
St. Peter
Lincoln Park
Florist Avenue
Peace
Wellington Park

Wisconsin Avenue:
Our Savior
St. Paul
Redeemer
Marquette campus
SeedFolks Youth
Mnistry

West:
Divine Word
Good Shepherd
Pentecost
Capitol Drive

East:
Bayshore
Kingo
UWM campus
Lake Park
Village

Organization of the Milwaukee Strategy

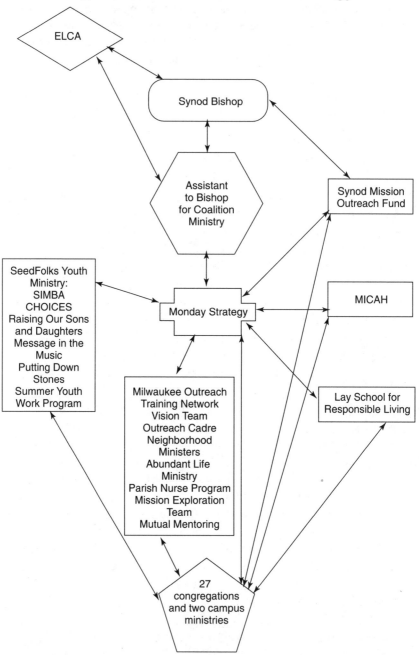

* The North, Far North, West, and Wisconsin Avenue are all in the Northwest quadrant of the city

Milwaukee Strategy, Wisconsin

The authors were very early for church on that first Sunday in Advent. With time to spare, we decided to find a store in the neighborhood to buy two cups of coffee. Up one street and down another, we saw plenty of boarded-up stores, dilapidated housing, and even a few abandoned houses. What we never did find was a place to buy coffee. We learned quickly that public services had deserted this neighborhood. There were almost no stores—clothing, grocery, or hardware—let alone a superstore like Kmart or Wal-Mart. There were no restaurants, not even a McDonalds or a Burger King, and no banks. Underfunded schools, liquor stores, and the churches were the only public presence left. That day we received a quick lesson about the importance of the church staying in neighborhoods like this one.

Without our coffee, on a cold winter morning with a biting wind blowing off Lake Michigan, we entered Hephatha Lutheran Church, where we encountered a warm haven in an uninviting environment. The warmth wasn't primarily because the furnace worked, but because of the reception we received from the 130 people at worship. Most of the faces we encountered were black, with cheerful smiles and words of greeting. Even more striking, the church was full of African-American children, including the three teenage girls who sat with us and made us feel comfortable.

The contrast was striking. On the one hand, Hephatha is located in one of the poorest and most depressing sections of Milwaukee's inner city. Yet in the church there was life, and hope and enthusiasm—a mood that fits the season of Advent, which anticipates a better future. It looks forward to Jesus' birth but also stirs expectation of what God might do in our futures. "Advent is rooted in the basic human longing for a better time."[1] Advent is to excite us with hope and strengthen us to trust a future to which God invites us.

Many questions came to our minds that Sunday morning. Where is hope in the desperate circumstances of the lives of many of the worshippers? To what kind of future can these children look forward? What future is there for badly addicted teenagers and adults? How can people hold realistic hope of escaping the cycle of poverty and despair?

One way that Hephatha and several other inner-city congregations address these issues is through a strong program for youth. At Hephatha, at every Sunday worship service, the children come forward to hear a message, to pray, and to recite a creed. On the Sunday we attended, from 50 to 60 children, ages 4 to 15, jammed the chancel. Some had a parent or guardian in church with them, a few had two parents, but many were there without parents—the church being the one oasis of hope in awful situations. Here is the creed they repeat after the pastor every Sunday and every Tuesday on their education night.

I am God's Child (x 3)
I may be rich
I may be poor
I may be exciting
I might be a bore
But I am God's child (x 2)

I may be black
I may be white
I may be free
I might be uptight
But I am God's child (x 2)

I may be yellow
I may be brown
I may be lost
I may be found
Mistreated
Unseated
But never defeated (x 2)

I am God's child (x 2)[2]

In the eagerness and enthusiasm of saying this creed, these children, we could see, had the message, "Because I'm God's child, and God's future beckons me, I'm never defeated." In this way the beginning of hope is given.

The primary reason Hephatha is a thriving congregation is that it is part of a corporate strategy that says the Evangelical Lutheran Church in America will not close its churches in Milwaukee's inner city. Instead, the ELCA will help turn these congregations into mission outreach posts to the neighborhood. The reason Hephatha is not an abandoned inner-city congregation is that a corporate model encouraged by the ELCA churchwide organization involves the Greater Milwaukee Synod (the regional expression of the ELCA), and includes partnerships with suburban congregations. Most particularly, both Hephatha's pastor and its people are nourished by a coalition of 32 outreach ministries, including 27 congregations gathered into the Milwaukee Strategy. At this point in its history portions of the pastor's salary and benefits are paid by a variety of sources, including the congregation, mission partners, and cooperating congregations in the Strategy. This chapter tells the remarkable story of a venture that has turned dying inner-city congregations into mission outposts to their neighborhoods.

Context

Milwaukee is a city of 610,000 people in a metropolitan area of 1.6 million. Located on Lake Michigan, it boasts major sports teams, major universities, and a focus on the arts.[3] Since reaching its population peak in 1960, the city of Milwaukee has lost 20.2 percent of its population, while the suburban population has increased by 61.3 percent. Comparing Milwaukee with 13 other Frost Belt cities, "no other city or metropolitan area approached the rate of decline in Milwaukee in real family income for blacks between 1970 and 1990.[4] No other Frost Belt city or metropolitan area approached Milwaukee's racial gap in the rate of family income growth during this period."[5] Black median family income in the Milwaukee area fell from 65.1 percent of white family income in 1970 to 39.5 percent in 1990. The poverty rate for blacks reached 41.2 percent in 1990, four times the white rate. In all these measures, Milwaukee ranked worst of the 14 cities.[6]

Moreover, in 1990, over 43 percent of city residents lived in census tracts in which at least one-fifth of the population fell below the poverty line. The proportion of blacks living in high-poverty neighborhoods rose from 8.4 percent in 1970 to 46.7 percent in 1990. Again, of the 14 cities metropolitan Milwaukee had the highest proportion of blacks living in high-poverty neighborhoods.[7]

Thus, Milwaukee "ranks worst among Frostbelt cities in the disparity between white and black poverty. By 1990, blacks in the city of Milwaukee were almost four times as likely as whites to live in poverty. . . . In each census year since 1970, the black-white poverty gap has been greater in Milwaukee than any other Frostbelt big city."[8] Also, unlike metropolitan areas like Baltimore and St. Louis, little suburbanization of blacks has occurred in Milwaukee.

> As a consequence of the well-documented metropolitan hyper-segregation here, even blacks who themselves are not poor are likely, to a greater degree in metropolitan Milwaukee than anywhere else in the Frostbelt, to live in neighborhoods where a high percentage of the population *is* poor. Thus, for almost half of all blacks in metropolitan Milwaukee in 1990, conditions of extreme poverty were a part of daily neighborhood life.[9]

There are 25 ELCA congregations in the city of Milwaukee and two campus ministries (Marquette University and the University of Wisconsin-Milwaukee). The majority of ELCA congregations in Milwaukee are in low- to lower-middle-income African-American neighborhoods. The poverty level (and hence the pressures of urban life) is compressed in Milwaukee because these pressures are concentrated geographically rather than dispersed. The remaining congregations are in changing neighborhoods in the "second ring" or "on the Avenue" (Wisconsin Avenue) or "near Southside." However, these changing neighborhoods suggest that they will continue to become more poverty-stricken in the future. Two congregations just outside the city limits join with the 25 city churches to form, along with the two campus ministries and three newly created specialized "outreach" ministries, the Milwaukee Strategy.

Development

The Rev. Richard Deines, assistant to the bishop of the Greater Milwaukee Synod and director of coalition ministry, has a passion for the corporate model of ministry. Says Rick Deines:

> In order to have corporate ministries, you have to have strong advocacy and clarity about that. As much passion as [pastors in this coalition bring to their congregations], I bring to the whole corporate model. We are working on building a new structural expression of the church at the local level. That is where my passion lies.

Deines and the pastors we spoke to in this cooperative are committed to an organic structure, one that grows and is ever-changing. Details about the exact shape of the cooperative at any point in the past are not very important to the people of this cooperative. In fact, the cooperative is formally a coalition of churches, but Rick Deines prefers the name "Milwaukee Strategy" because it suggests a cooperative that is more flexible and less fixed. However, corporate models for Lutheran churches in Milwaukee do have a long history.

Pastor Deines himself had served congregations of the former Lutheran Church in America in urban Chicago and Kansas City (1975-1981) and has been leading coalition ministry in Milwaukee since 1981, originally serving as coordinator for the LCA congregations organized into the "Milwaukee Area Ministry." The American Lutheran Church (ALC) had its own full-time director in a coalition of ALC urban congregations, called "The Milwaukee Urban Parish." The Lutheran merger of 1987 united the LCA, the ALC, and the Association of Evangelical Lutheran Churches (AELC—formerly part of the Lutheran Church–Missouri Synod) into the Evangelical Lutheran Church in America (ELCA). With the merger of these bodies into one church, the size and the scope of the cooperative ministry became much greater.

There were many highlights of cooperative ministry prior to the 1987 merger. In 1983 the Milwaukee Area Ministry began to serve a Friday evening meal at Reformation Lutheran Church to assist the congregation in linking with its immediate community. More than ten ELCA congregations together serve 200 to 300 people a week. In 1984 Habitat for Humanity was initiated in Milwaukee by the LCA coalition. More than 125 families now live in Habitat for Humanity housing. In 1986 the ALC's "Urban Parish" and the LCA's "Milwaukee Area Ministry," plus congregations from the AELC, formed the pan-Lutheran Milwaukee Area Lutheran Coalition with a staff of three (including Rick Deines). In 1986, 30 people of color began to participate in a two-year training program for congregational lay leaders, called the Academy for Ministry Preparation. The pan-Lutheran coalition created an alternative worship service and resource piece called "Celebrate CommUNITY" in 1987.

The ELCA was born in 1987, and the Rev. Peter Rogness was elected synod bishop. Rogness had been a pastor for ten years at Hephatha Lutheran Church. From the time of his election, Bishop Rogness has provided strong leadership and effective advocacy for urban congregations, pastors, and the corporate model. He named Rick Deines to the full-time position as assistant to the bishop for coalition ministry.

During a retreat of city pastors and lay leaders held shortly after the merger, those assembled divided the ministry in the city of Milwaukee into four strategy areas: Northside, Southside, Wisconsin Avenue, and Eastside (Lakeside). These strategy areas were projected as mission cluster arenas for congregations to work together more effectively in their neighborhoods. At the time these strategies were formed, the Northside area was where the Lutheran churches were sited amid the most serious poverty. From this new formation, ministries began to blossom. It has become an organic model that is always changing while holding onto key basic foundations. Pastor Deines describes it as the "loose tight principle."[10] It means "you have direction but you aren't wedded to it and you're willing to shift as things indicate. It's more like an accordion effect organizationally than it is a straight line."

Ministries

1. Northside Strategy/Monday Strategy

The Northside Strategy has become the glue that holds the Milwaukee Coalition together. Says Rick Deines:

> The most important thing about the Monday Strategy is that it's met without fail for over ten years, every single week. And there have been a couple of holidays where the number was small, but

with these rare exceptions, there have been 25 to 30 people every single week. It's mostly for the commitment of the clergy and laity who really believe that the corporate model works best.

The Strategy session meets every Monday from noon until 2 P.M. The first hour is a Bible study on the texts for the next Sunday's worship, always focusing the text on the concrete situation of the neighborhoods in which the churches are located; i.e., neighborhood people, especially the poor and the marginalized. The Bible study is followed by a brief communion service. The second hour focuses on issues for the city churches and the sharing of resources, directions, and concerns.

The Northside Strategy began as one of four strategies involving ten congregations but has evolved into *the* weekly strategy session for the whole city, with participation from most of the 27 congregations in the coalition. The other strategies still meet with greater or lesser frequency. However, pastors and lay leaders from all over the city come to the Northside Strategy. Deines has now started calling it the "Monday Strategy," although we noticed that some of the pastors and leaders still call it Northside Strategy.

Why did the Northside Strategy become the glue that holds the whole coalition together? First, the Lutheran churches in the most desperate neighborhoods were, and still are, within the Northside area of Milwaukee. Second, key Lutheran congregations located in Northside have strong, experienced urban pastors and congregations with strong outreach to the community. Three congregations and pastors in particular bear mention here.

The Rev. Joseph Ellwanger has been an urban pastor since 1958. He served nine years (1958-1967) in Birmingham, Alabama, where he "cut his eyeteeth" in urban ministry and on the road to Selma. That is, in Birmingham with Dr. Martin Luther King, Jr., and others, he learned (1) that urban ministry is ecumenical ministry (which enabled him "to emerge out of the walls the Lutheran Church–Missouri Synod pastors tend to remain in"), and (2) that urban ministry is justice ministry. Joe Ellwanger says that doing justice is not a back-burner concern but "is part and parcel of a proclamation and a living of the Gospel. It is not in spite of the Gospel that we do justice but because of the Gospel, and as a sign of the Gospel and witness to the Gospel."

Ellwanger was called to be pastor of Cross Lutheran Church in 1967 and has been there ever since, developing one of the most faithful and effective urban congregations in Milwaukee. Pastor Ellwanger and Cross

Church were part of the Lutheran Church–Missouri Synod and then the AELC until 1987, when his "official" connection with the Lutheran coalition began. For years the Cross congregation worked primarily alone—not in an isolationist sense, but as a church on the frontier and in the vanguard, setting an example for others in the city. Ellwanger is an invaluable resource and teacher for the entire Milwaukee coalition.

The Rev. Edgar "Mick" Roschke is pastor of Reformation Lutheran Church. Pastor Roschke was serving as the "community minister" at Sherman Park Lutheran Church when Rick Deines came to Milwaukee from Kansas City in 1981. Deines set up his office first at Reformation Lutheran Church and later in a storefront on North Avenue, which also housed the S.O.S. Center, a street ministry that Roschke had started. Part of their initial vision was to create a Stephen Ministries model for churches in the city. Roschke was a quarter-time national trainer for this ministry in addition to his work at Sherman Park. The Stephen Ministries focus on teaching laypeople about empowerment for one-on-one caring ministries. The two of them started meeting with Jean Leslie, an active Lutheran lay member, who is now executive director of Milwaukee Habitat for Humanity. The work that was catalyzed by this relationship included the local Habitat for Humanity, a Lutheran program for outreach training for 300 people called "Word and Witness," the Academy for Ministry Preparation, and Going Public, an immersion in city life to help suburban church people overcome their fear of the city.

Reformation provides another model for urban ministry. Because of visionary pastoral leadership before Roschke came, according to Deines,

> Reformation, more than any other congregation I know, kept the old congregation involved, according to Rick, when it went in a radically new direction. They learned the importance of being the church at their location, and the importance of giving their resources for [the] neighborhood. This congregation didn't lose its financial backing, and the building did not fall into the kind of disrepair that most do.

The new direction of ministry blossomed under Roschke, of whom Deines says, "I don't think I've ever met a human being who is as good one-on-one as Mick is in terms of personal caring." Now the leader of the Outreach Cadre, Mick Roschke has written a book titled *A Church of the People: Strategies of Urban Ministry.*[11]

The third influential pastor is the Rev. Dennis Jacobson at Incarnation Lutheran Church. "Jake" Jacobson has been pastor of this church for over 11 years. He heads the church-based organizing effort of the coalition, by leading the Lutheran congregational involvement in MICAH (Milwaukee Inner-city Congregations Allied for Hope). He is also national director of the Clergy Caucus for the Gamaliel Foundation, the training organization for MICAH. The Gamaliel Foundation is a church-based community-organizing training laboratory. According to Rick Deines, Pastor Jacobson is the key theological trainer for Gamaliel, nationwide. "Church-based organizing has always been a little short on theological grounding. Now Jake is writing the manual."

With these three pastors, the Northside Strategy became the vanguard of cooperative ministry, a place where pastors from the other strategies started coming. As one participant in the Monday Strategy put it, people come

> because: (1) the agenda includes vibrant Bible study in which questions and examples are very helpful in dealing with the reality of urban persons' lives; and (2) issues we pick up during the second hour are very helpful to us pastors; and (3) strong gifted pastors with a lot to offer sit at that table so there is a sense of learning from pastors who have not only talked the talk but walked the walk for many years. Jake, Mick, and Joe are a rare combination not to be found many places.

All new pastors in the coalition are invited and encouraged immediately to attend the Monday Strategy, and in recent years, almost all have. This weekly meeting is the cauldron out of which many new ministry directions have been forged, where mutual mentoring has occurred, and where leaders simultaneously come for support and to be held accountable. Without the Monday Strategy, the coalition might not dissolve completely, but it would not have the depth and breadth of investment in the neighborhoods that it has.

All of the pastors and laypeople at the Monday Strategy bring their own gifts to the work of the coalition. As with any group, the Strategy struggles at times to include everyone in the planning and ownership of the work. One-third of the group is made up of women, who for a time formed a "women's cadre" to deal with special issues that were not being addressed in the larger group. Spanish-speaking, Hmong, African-American, and Native American pastors and lay leaders bring special gifts that are not always effectively integrated into the work of the Strategy. The Monday Strategy continues to work on these concerns in the larger framework of the coalition.

Soon after its formation, the Northside Strategy began to work on a set of "Givens of Outreach Strategy." By "givens," the group means that these elements should be in place in all coalition churches for mutual ministry and effective mission. As stated in the recent paper written by Rick Deines, the "givens" are as follows:

1.   Nurturing youth through a summer program, youth academy, and after-school program [and today SIMBA, CHOICES, Name that Music].

2.   Empowering adults through outreach cadre, MICAH training and participation, cross-cultural staffing, economic development, and the lay school for responsible living.

3.   Developing partnerships through congregation redevelopment or new starts, through city-suburban-rural relationship and funding resource development.

4.   Building ministry teams through [an] overall team as "strategy staff," through strategy groups throughout the city, through the Milwaukee Outreach Training Network and through ELCA support/participation.

5.   Creating contextual worship opportunities through weekly liturgy shaped locally, through Word and Sacrament focus, through the centrality of scripture, and through daily life emphasis on mission and faith.[12]

One issue in the coalition is that more than half the current pastors were not part of the Milwaukee Strategy when the "givens" were formulated. This factor has caused minor friction. For example, the pastors who developed the "givens" think that most (but not all) congregations in the coalition should belong to MICAH. In fact, only seven congregations are members of MICAH, and most seem reluctant to join—not because they don't believe in the tenets of MICAH, but because they don't have the personal energy or the leadership pool in their congregation to stretch in one further direction in their ministry. Even the $700 minimum annual gift to belong to MICAH is difficult for some struggling inner-city congregations. Nevertheless, the "givens" stand as goals for all congregations engaged in the coalition.

2. MICAH

Even before the "givens" were fully sketched out by the Northside Strategy, pastors of the Strategy were instrumental in the formation of MICAH, an ecumenical organization that began in 1989. Milwaukee Inner-city Congregations Allied for Hope (MICAH) is part of a network called the Gamaliel Foundation, headquartered in Chicago.

According to Pastor Jacobson, there are four church-based organizing networks in the United States. Gamaliel relates to 40 organizations like MICAH in 11 states, and there are emerging organizations in South Africa as well. About 1,000 congregations are part of Gamaliel. *One-on-One Training*, a Milwaukee Strategy program, provides training primarily through the Gamaliel Foundation. "This involves learning how to converse with persons in such a way that their own self-interest is identified and they can feel some inclination to become involved in issues facing the neighborhood and the city."[13] As a part of this program, a longer eight-day training is held near Chicago by the Gamaliel Foundation, where many clergy and laity of this cooperative have been trained.

MICAH itself is made up of 36 city congregations and one suburban, a Lutheran congregation that entered MICAH through a partnership arrangement with Reformation and Incarnation churches. MICAH addresses issues of importance to residents of the city, as well as participating in holding business, police, government, schools, and other officials accountable for quality of life in Milwaukee. During the authors' visit to Milwaukee, we attended a semi-annual MICAH public meeting, where 400-plus people jammed into a church designed to hold fewer. At this meeting, MICAH was confronting and working with governmental officials and private industry on three key issues.

The first was transportation, as MICAH sought to have public transportation routes added from inner-city Milwaukee to key places of employment in the county. Second, MICAH was pressing to maintain funding for AODA (Alcohol and Other Drug Addiction) treatment. The money available for uninsured people seeking treatment has shrunk steadily, even as the need has increased. MICAH has long challenged the government of Milwaukee County to keep AODA treatment as a priority—at least as important as a new stadium, a museum, or lakefront roadways. Third, MICAH was lobbying to have smaller teacher-pupil ratios through a program called SAGE. With large classes, SAGE (Student Achieved Guaranteed Education) would add a second teacher to a classroom. This effort means lobbying Wisconsin state officials.[14]

According to Jacobson, MICAH has enormous potential. "We're starting to think more and more regionally, and even statewide. . . . When we started, the issues were very local. We were dealing with the mayor a lot, and with the aldermen. Now it's really with the county supervisors or with the state level of government. In order to do that, we need a lot more power." So Jacobson talks about their efforts to develop a regional coalition, cooperating with organizations in the suburbs and in neighboring cities.

Jacobson admits that there is a risk in this effort. Greater Milwaukee is a place of great racial separation. MICAH is making history in being able to form an organization in which black and white pastors work together. "As we draw in more and more suburban congregations, we run the risk of losing the black church[es], as they may perceive it becoming a white-dominated organization." Finally, Jacobson described MICAH's focus. "MICAH is a power organization, and we do not do development work or a training program. We might, however, force the funding of these things with an agency."

3. Youth Outreach

In 1989, Venice Williams White was called by Cross Lutheran Church and the Milwaukee Coalition as youth director. White, a graduate of Valparaiso University and a former member of the Lutheran Church–Missouri Synod, worked for eight years with her dual responsibilities. However, her role in the coalition kept growing, and as long as she was at Cross, she could not give the coalition ministry the focused attention it needed. In June 1997, she became director of the *SeedFolks Youth Ministry*. According to White, SeedFolks is "a ministry that's created specifically to develop the youth for leadership in the city churches."

Venice Williams White says that there is not enough money to go around and therefore not enough staffing to have a paid youth leader in every congregation. Therefore, "my role is to create models and do training events, to be the ministry that helps the city congregations to create *healthy* youth ministries." One of her chief tasks is to train lay leaders. She now has a second layperson hired to work with her in youth ministry. White has instituted the following programs for youth.

SIMBA Circle Ministry is an outreach ministry specifically directed to African-American males, ages eight to 18, who live in the inner city. The SIMBA Circle holds meetings monthly during the year. Started five years ago in Milwaukee, SIMBA Circle is now a national ELCA ministry. It began with a two-week camp in summer 1993 held between Chicago and Milwaukee. Venice White is not only national chair for SIMBA Circle; she also trains people nationally to lead a SIMBA Circle in their own urban areas. In August, SIMBA Circle Ministry completed its fifth camp, with about 160 African-American males attending. The Milwaukee coalition sent 40 of the youth. White noted, with a smile, the irony that she is an African-American woman heading a national program for African-American boys and young men.

CHOICES is a ministry for urban girls. It began when Venice White took a group of middle-schools girls to a movie, "and they came back to my house and told horror stories of what it's like to be a middle-school girl." So "we decided that the church needs to create a safe place for girls to explore who they are and all the changes they are going through." They began the program with a weeklong camp attended by 30 girls. Now four training events are held every year for congregations in the Milwaukee coalition. At these events White trains local leaders to lead SIMBA Circle or CHOICES groups. At least two adult leaders are required from a congregation. The CHOICES groups can be for elementary-age girls, or middle-school, or both middle-school and high-school girls. CHOICES groups for adults are parenting groups for those with girls in these age categories. Because CHOICES has grown so much, White is in the process of writing a curriculum for it.

The model for CHOICES is a weekly sit-down family dinner with china. "Like any family, this is the arena where all the issues come out." Venice has 18 students from Marquette who have been assigned to work with her in service learning. "What happens is that they go through CHOICES, and they don't leave because they've never had anything like this." The CHOICES group is most fully developed at Redeemer Church, where White has her offices. "On any given Tuesday there will be 20 to 50 females from age ten to 35. After they eat together, they break out in small groups."

When girls enter CHOICES, parents and guardians sign a covenant with White. She then writes a letter to the student's school saying that this girl is in CHOICES. The school contacts her if there is reason to celebrate or to be concerned. White receives copies of every report card. If girls are suspended, they are referred to White. Moreover, the involvement in local school is wider than just Venice White. The Milwaukee Strategy emphasizes that churches need to be immersed in the school nearest to the parish. Reformation Church, for example, offers a Peace Award each year and hosts an annual Affirmation Dinner at nearby Washington High School.

Almost as an afterthought, White told us an important fact she had just realized. While CHOICES does not focus on teenage pregnancy, in five years, among the girls who have come regularly, there have been no pregnancies. Such a statistic has to be one barometer of the effectiveness of CHOICES, especially since Milwaukee has one of the highest percentages of teen pregnancies in the nation.

Raising Our Sons and Daughters grew out of CHOICES. It was created in 1997 as an effort to bring in some of the mothers and grandmothers. About half the youth who come regularly to SIMBA or CHOICES are being raised by their grandmothers, since their mothers are addicted to drugs or alcohol. This ministry was started for students who participate at the church in creative, helpful programs, but then go home to a dysfunctional environment, where often no adult is working, and parents are on alcohol and drugs. This has become a very personal ministry; White spends much time in the kids' homes. After White visits with the parent or guardian several times in the homes, the mothers or grandmothers come to Raising our Sons and Daughters, and the children go to CHOICES or SIMBA.

Message in the Music was born when White was at home watching music videos and exclaimed, "I can't believe this stuff." The model is again a family meal that meets monthly. White says that the meal gets them there the first time, but the ministry keeps them there. They decipher the message in these songs. They write in their journals about it. After two months White says, "We've listened to what you listen to, and we will continue to do it, but now you also have to listen to what we listen to." After four months or so, the youth started writing their own lyrics. Venice gave them topics like "Tell Me Your Story of Life in the City," and asked them to write a rap song. Soon they were writing songs and changing them into liturgies. Now a public school has opened up its recording facilities, and the youth have written two worship services. The long-range plan is to create liturgies that can be related to a congregation. According to White, the programs reach different audiences—the girls who come to CHOICES do not come to Message in the Music, and vice versa.

Putting Down Stones is a monthly experience that pulls together suburban and urban youth leaders. Most of the confirmation classes incorporate Putting Down Stones. White arranges the opportunity for them to come together and talk about racial issues or current events from their different perspectives. Eucharist is offered at the end of an evening of Putting Down Stones.

In addition there are the *summer youth work programs* that involve youth in daily work over several weeks during the summer. Youth undertake neighborhood work projects and are paid a modest wage for their efforts. These young people are required to attend Sunday worship as part of the discipline of the work program. By the end of summer, they have saved enough money to buy new clothes to begin the school year.

4. Milwaukee Outreach Training Network

Officially formed in 1994, the Milwaukee Outreach Training Network (MOTN) "is the training arm of the Milwaukee Lutheran Coalition/Strategy. Its purpose is to provide training and strategic resources for the professional and lay leadership of 27 congregations, its mission partners, two campus ministries and three experimental outreach ministries in the Milwaukee area."[15]

MOTN immediately created a *Vision Team*, meeting monthly, to provide direction and accountability. The team is made up of lay and clergy professionals who head specific ministries of the coalition: Jake Jacobson for church-based organizing, Mick Roschke for Outreach Cadre, Tom Shaffer for Abundant Life, Jean Miller for neighborhood ministers, Venice White for youth, and others bringing to the table concern for relationships with African-Americans, American Indians, Asian-Americans, Spanish-speaking Americans, gay and lesbian people, suburban partners, and seminaries. According to Rick Deines, "We have 15 or 16 people who form the Vision Team, and any one of their ministries can exist on its own, but when you bring all of them in relationship with one another, then all sorts of wonderful things happen." The Vision Team also functions when necessary as a "board" for funding purposes and to make recommendations to the synod council. A smaller group from the Vision Team meets every two weeks to deal with day-to-day operations and coordination.

The *Outreach Cadre*, now a part of MOTN, was formed in 1991. Headed by Mick Roschke, this group, with some clergy but mostly laypeople, meets monthly for 90-minute training sessions in specialized areas of neighborhood outreach. The cadre participants are teamed to make visits in a neighborhood and learn about how to deal with addicted residents, and others with chronic needs. The cadre trains by visiting the neighborhood around one church for a period of time and then moving on to another location. Currently, for a two-year period the cadre will be visiting in the neighborhood surrounding a church that is trying to get started in neighborhood ministry (see ABCD Ministries).

Neighborhood Ministers has been a critical addition to the Milwaukee Coalition. The concept of a neighborhood minister originated with Mick Roschke at Reformation. He realized that because he was an outsider, there were certain places and family homes to which he would never be invited. But someone who was "local," who had lived in the neighborhood for many years and suffered some of the same traumas, could go to these areas of need. So the church hired a local parishioner with a strong relationship to the church and leadership potential to become the neighborhood minister.

Jean Miller was hired as the first neighborhood minister in 1993. She told the authors that her job is different every day. She doesn't talk about ministering *to* people or serving them; rather her language is consistently "walking with them." She visits people in the neighborhood. She lets them know about the food pantry, emergency clothing, the parish nurse. She "walks with" people with addictions, with illnesses such as AIDS, and those without food or heat. She also shares her faith openly, not only in the neighborhood, but also on educational nights at church when she teaches. Because she has five children herself, she knows many of the children and teenagers in the neighborhood. When people come for help, they used to see the pastor, but now they come see "Ms. Miller." At first people resisted not seeing the pastor, but he always sent them to her, and now it's OK, she says. She also regularly visits nursing homes. There are now five neighborhood ministers in the coalition, with hopes that, given additional funding, there can be many more.

MOTN developed a career-development ministry that has now evolved into *Abundant Life Ministry*. The ministry director is Tom Shaffer, whom Deines describes as "an emerging lay theologian." The seeds were planted in 1991, when Shaffer came from Chicago to Milwaukee because his wife is an ELCA pastor who took a position in the coalition. An urban developer by training, Shaffer was hired by a nonprofit agency to start an employment program that went very well. Shaffer needed a trusted labor pool for the employment opportunities, so he turned to ELCA congregations. That drew him into the coalition, and he began attending the Monday Strategy meetings.

His own religious reawakening occurred in this process.

> Participating in the Bible studies and hanging out with the pastors, I began to really get into the Jesus story . . . and my life was coming more and more together as I was embracing the Jesus story. If this works for me, we should be integrating Jesus' story into our work with job applicants.

Shaffer was originally hired by the coalition to give 10 percent of his time for job placement in the coalition. Then in early 1997, he was called to his position as lay minister in career development, making him a full-time outreach worker within the coalition.

Abundant Life Ministry has two primary components: career development and neighborhood development. Shaffer and others work directly with pastors and congregations, both to prepare inner-city residents so that they are ready to assume full-time work and to locate appropriate jobs for them. Shaffer equates his job to that of a vocational counselor. But he is quick to point out that he speaks in theological terms of people having vocations from God. Much of his theological reading is in the area of theological vocation. God's story and the church are integrally connected in Shaffer's work.

Shaffer hastens to point out that Abundant Life is first and foremost an outreach ministry of the synod to build ELCA churches. "It happens to be that we turn into an excellent job-placement program, but that is not where we start. So we are an outreach ministry and an 'in-reach' ministry. We know the people because the pastor knows the people." Abundant Life Ministry does find jobs for people in the neighborhoods who do not belong to any of the coalition churches. However, job applicants from the neighborhoods without a church home are invited to participate in a coalition church's ministry. Eighty percent of those placed have joined one of the coalition churches. At one time, the coalition considered setting up Abundant Life Ministry as an independent nonprofit organization, but to keep itself clearly tied to coalition outreach, Abundant Life is now accountable within the Greater Milwaukee Synod structure. That connection is reflected in proposals now reviewed and approved by the Synod Council.

Since about half the people Shaffer works with have a history of alcohol and drug problems and many others have no experience in applying for a job, his work is labor-intensive, involving extensive one-on-one work. The track record has been good. First, Shaffer is honest with employers in conveying as much as he knows about the person that might affect job performance. Second, statistics show that Abundant Life has a commendable track record of job retention. According to Shaffer, "In Milwaukee, the average for job retention—that is, people still employed by the company after six months—is 50 percent. Our retention rate at six months is 71 percent." Seventy percent of the people Shaffer places are African-Americans.

Shaffer works not only with inner-city churches but also with partner churches in the suburbs, because that is where many of the employers are. Abundant Life has its own fund-raiser. That is, Shaffer's offices are located at Reformation Lutheran Church; that church hires a fund-raiser half-time, and Abundant Life purchases her services for the other half. Grants, Shaffer says, are available for programs that are putting people to work. Since 1992, he has helped place almost 650 people in jobs.

The *Parish Nurse* program exists because there is inadequate medical care in the inner city and little money to go to doctors. When you work with people in the inner city, says Mick Roschke, you have to keep coming back to them, because they often are active for a while and then drop out, often because they've relapsed and resumed their addictions. "But we keep inviting them back. Many of the people are addicted to booze and cocaine. This is why our parish nurse is such a wonderful ministry." Reformation Church teams with Incarnation Church so that the parish nurse is in each church three days a week. The parish nurse sometimes makes visits with the neighborhood minister. Fifteen congregations now have a parish nurse at least part-time. In the future the Milwaukee Strategy would like to have parish nurses available for all congregations in the coalition.

Mission Exploration Teams are people from other congregations in the city who join with a team from the local church to dream and point to future possibilities for ministry from that local church. While the authors were in Milwaukee, a Mission Exploration Team was meeting to work on a call process during a congregation's pastoral search. The chair of the exploration team was the pastor of one of the other congregations in the Strategy.

Together, those inside the church and those from other coalition churches developed a vision of what future mission might emerge in that congregation.

The professional leaders in the Strategy commit themselves to work with each other in the ministry they share, called *Mutual Mentoring*. A variety of forms exist, from one-on-one conversations to up to five people meeting regularly to share issues of life and ministry. Mick Roschke says that one of the real joys of being in a cooperative is Mutual Mentoring. "When a new pastor is called to the city, she or he is teamed with an experienced pastor." Actually, the new pastor chooses the pastor he or she would prefer as a mentor. "But it's not like the veteran pastor training the rookie, but it is mutual mentoring, so that we are learning from one another." Roschke has been meeting with two other coalition pastors for five years for deep sharing, support, and prayer.

One of the most ambitious and promising ministry initiatives undertaken by the Strategy is the *Lay School for Responsible Living*. This school is a primary tool to identify and train lay leaders for their local churches and community. It's about lay empowerment. According to Joy True, one of the chairs of this ministry, the first steps toward a lay school were taken when Rick Deines had the seed of an idea. "Let's do something for the laity, the lay leaders in congregations. Let's develop their skills and their gifts, support them as they grow in their faith, and then move them back to congregations to do wondrous things."

Begun in 1996, the school meets in the spring and the fall each year on four successive Monday nights. Additional courses are offered on Saturdays. "The purpose of the lay school is to train lay persons for a variety of outreach which exists using the gifts the participant brings to ministry."[16] The basic orientation course, which must be taken first, is "In the City for Good." Then courses are offered in five areas: theology, Bible, outreach, "Spiritual Journey," and "The Times and the Gospel." While some group leaders have been church professionals, including Bishop Peter Rogness and Professor Jim Bailey from Wartburg Lutheran Seminary, the leaders are predominantly laypeople from the Milwaukee Coalition.

A certificate as a "Lay Worker in Ministry" is given to participants who complete a two-year course by taking the "In the City for Good" orientation plus four other classes. "'Lay Worker in Specialized Ministry' is for those wanting special mentoring in the areas of outreach with the neighborhood, youth, work ministry, career development, and so forth."[17] The certificate for a "Lay Worker in Specialized Ministry" is tailored to individuals and is usually completed sometime after the Lay Worker in Ministry

Certification is earned. "Lay Certification is an agreement between the person and the congregation that a commitment has been made to leadership in the congregation. Specialization makes that commitment specific in an area of church life."[18]

The goal of the lay school is to have 2,000 lay leaders trained by the year 2020. According to Joy True, a good mixture of races attends the school. Moreover, some are just starting the journey in the Christian faith and don't have the background or the history of the Lutheran church. This is an opportunity to grow in many areas. However, it's done "by walking with each other on the journey. And this journey starts with God's grace and the assurance God loves you as you are, and affirms that he's given us each gifts. So, let's help each other find out what those gifts are." Joy True, one of the co-leaders of the lay school, is an unpaid volunteer who works full time at a secular job.

Vision

The vision of the Milwaukee Strategy is a corporate one. The vision is formed not only by the pastors and laity in these congregations, but also through coalitions with the ELCA, the synod bishop's office and other outside groups like MICAH. Rick Deines is not so much the *creator* of the vision (although he is one of the main sources) as he is the *keeper* of the vision, through his leadership style.

Deines's leadership style became apparent to the authors by the way he scheduled our visit to Milwaukee. We thought we would start by interviewing him, learn his perspective on this cooperative, and then interview all the other leaders to hear their stories. Instead, Pastor Deines very carefully set up a schedule for us and met with us at various steps along the way to make sure there were no problems. But he insisted that we interview everyone else first. We heard the vision from others. Only then did he sit down to be interviewed. His first words were, "I always figure that if I've done my job, this is going to be a very short interview. You've heard it all from the other staff. You asked me to tell you about our Strategy, and I simply had you go talk to the staff and parishioners and make up your own minds about what this coalition is."

In Deines's spirit, the authors will begin with what others said about his leadership in the Strategy and amplify these comments with his own insights. Asked how important Deines's role is for the coalition, one pastor responded,

> His ministry is totally important. Unless you have somebody on the bishop's staff who gives all of his energy to this coalition, then it easily would not happen. Without someone like him, it would never get started or be held together. Without him, you fall into, "Well, I'm so busy here. I'm not going to meet with this outside group or that resource person. I won't meet with people on Mondays."

Deines says of himself,

> My job is running interference. When they wander from the vision for a while, I call them back to it. The reason the vision stays central is that that's my task. My task is to continue to focus people on that which is beyond themselves. As much as they are invested in their own place, except in a few instances, they can't be completely involved in what is happening in other places. That's the way it has to be. They need a vehicle so that learnings can be shared and cooperation increased across the cluster.

Another pastor said,

> He's our mutual mentor, but he's also someone who is a "creative outsider" because he doesn't have a congregation and he can continuously call you into accountability. He's so good. He's not an office person. He's with the pastors and leaders all week long, and he walks with you in a strong advocacy way. He's an avid reader, so he stretches you into looking at things in a new way.

That is to say, Deines is a possibility thinker whose basic stance is, "Let's try it." As Jacobson puts it,

> Rick is amazingly resourceful. I have never seen him shoot down an idea. He never comes in with judgments. He's always encouraging and supportive. As a director, he's a sort of pastor to pastors here. That's of great value. He's very intelligent, very creative, very resourceful. And he supports opening up doors.

In the orientation course to the Lay School for Responsible Living, a basic insight taught is to "go outside the box." The school uses the familiar technique of having each person connect nine dots in a square in four straight lines without lifting the pen. The only way one can successfully complete this task is to go outside the block of dots. This exercise epitomizes Deines's whole approach: encouragement and support to try new things and not worry about the structure.

One specific example of Deines's leadership style is the ministry at Redeemer Church. This congregation is too small to afford a full-time minister, but in a changing neighborhood, it has a clear vision of what its purpose is in that location. Rick approached a laywoman—a lawyer and president of her suburban congregation in probably the richest county in Wisconsin (a Milwaukee suburb)—and asked her if she would undertake the leader position at Redeemer. Ellen Maxon said yes.

Maxon had been a synod council member, active in the Strategy, and with a master's degree in social work as well as a law degree, committed to social justice. Ellen Maxon agreed on a trial basis to work at Redeemer half-time. When we interviewed her, we learned that she feels called to this position. Moreover, she is quite willing to keep her law practice small and, in fact, has moved her office back to her home so that she doesn't have overhead expense. Says Maxon: "The good thing is the bishop and Rick are willing to take that kind of risk." She thought it was good to be "tied to a system—Greater Milwaukee Synod, [Bishop] Peter [Rogness], and Rick—that is not so tied to procedure that it keeps you from moving ahead or doing ministry. You can easily get so stuck in procedural stuff or administration that you never move ahead." As a layperson, she does not consecrate the elements or perform baptisms or marriages, but in all other respects she is pastor of this congregation. Asking Ellen Maxon to fill this ministry need is one of the many ways Deines colors outside the box.

Deines says,

> Narrative is part of leadership. You [as director] transcend all that's going on. You hold out the open end to all of this, pointing out that the vision is going somewhere. That helps cohere. You are weaving a story. I think most people would think of me, "The future's wide open; let's do it." In the church we have a lot of people giving reasons why we shouldn't do it, can't do it, won't do it, but not many saying, "Let's do it."

Deines is not tied to structure. He says they've had a thousand different structures, but that's not important because structures in this coalition are "very fluid, very informal." What is important is that the structure be organic and that ministry continues to grow in areas that matter.

On the other hand, Deines does have a *Consultation Table Manual*, more than four inches thick, with detailed descriptions of each ministry, maps, demographics, data on the congregations, financial projections for the next five years, and dreams of where new ministries might be started. All the structure is there and spelled out, but no one seems chained by the present structure.

Another crucial aspect of Deines's leadership is, in his words: "We never use lack of money to say, 'We would embark on this ministry if we just had the money.'" Rick Deines sees one of his most important responsibilities as finding the money.

> This is a very risky thing to say, but I think we really have the money for whatever we want to do as the church. And I think we just have to find it. I'm amazed at the hidden sources for funding that are out there. . . . We're going on 18 years here, and we've never had a money problem with all we want to do, and we've started all these ministries.

Deines goes on to say how hard they work for money and how generously people are willing to give money, but "it is just the fact that we always find the money somehow." If a pastor wants to go to a national workshop on spirituality but can't find money elsewhere, Deines finds the money and she goes. If a congregation is in desperate need for money to hire a neighborhood minister, Deines finds the money to hire her part-time. When a pastor wants and needs a six-week sabbatical, Deines steps in and fills the pulpit for six weeks. As one coalition pastor said of him, "Because he's in conversation with all the congregations, if one has a special need, he brings it to us and it's more likely to happen than if the pastor herself brought it to the table."

According to his peers, Rick Deines is a very able theologian. He acknowledges the importance of theology by saying, "I think one of my strengths is a real theological undergirding of the vision. I don't just choose ministry directions for the sake of choosing them, but I choose what best reflects the values of the Gospel . . . in terms of that which brings life or prevents life from happening." Given this theological grounding, which insists on solidarity with the poor, "he gets us off dead center when we get bogged down," said one pastor.

At one point Deines described his job as "keeping the beat for the music." From the context of his remarks, "keeping the beat" means keeping the coalition focused on the vision and holding the vision together. Then Rick Deines says he has three principles that are really key. First, "if you're going to have an effective organization, have key decision-makers frequently around the table talking with one another." Second is the "loose tight principle" of having a direction but not being slavishly wedded to it. He calls the third principle "stick to your knitting"—that is, keep focused on your main vision: outreach neighborhood ministry.[19]

To keep the whole vision together and workable, Deines is able to deal with many levels of commitment to the wider Milwaukee ministry. For example, some pastors, whose churches are in MICAH, are impatient that other congregations are not joining MICAH. Deines can deal with this difference. "It's a stance of trying to honor everybody's journey and knowing the vision is long-termed enough and multifaceted enough that when pastors come and don't fully join in, still they have been able to find in this context a way of exercising their gifts for ministry."

Deines did not try to spell out his vision for us in detail. Instead he asked us to look around and examine what is happening here and let that be a vision of a corporate model of congregational ministry. In print, however, he has spelled out that vision to various audiences: the ELCA Division for Outreach, the synod, granting agencies, and the leaders of the Milwaukee Coalition. None of these visions is exactly the same, but they all have the same core. At the heart of all the visions is giving life to people in the name of Jesus Christ.

Tensions

The tensions in this cooperative seem muted, perhaps because the ministry situations are so spiritually, emotionally, and physically draining that coming together for help and mutual support is a necessity. There are plenty of tensions within congregations, of course, especially in those congregations that are trying to turn their ministry around to be outreach based in the neighborhood.

Being an urban pastor is difficult work, and even with the support of the coalition and Rick Deines, only three pastors have been in place longer than 11 years. One of Deines's own self-critiques (not heard from any of the leaders we interviewed) is that some pastors being thrust into the urban scene need a lot of ongoing "hand-holding."

> I have to admit that I'm not the person to do that myself. If you need personal hand-holding, then we can figure it out with people in the coalition. My efforts are to put you in community with other pastors and leaders, make sure you have a salary and a housing allowance. None of that would be there without structural care. If there is a critique of me personally, I think it would be that I'm not the warm, fuzzy, one-on-one person. I don't mean I'm not personable, because I think I am.

Second, there is an inevitable subtle tension between the pastors in the coalition against which the Strategy contends continually with some success. Mick Roschke put it this way, "The rough part sometimes is that in all of our enthusiasm—for example about the 'givens,' others can view this as demands. They may perceive that if I'm not doing this, then I am less of a pastor. And so we have to keep encouraging one another."

Several pastors told us that it takes new people a while to catch on to the Strategy and its way of support. They are used to a straight pastoral-care model. They are not really trained to empower laity and to equip people, and often not trained to work together with other people. "So when you come into a group like this, it's very invigorating, but it's also new, and there are some rubs once in a while," said one pastor.

African-American pastors, women, and pastors new to the Strategy can feel isolated and ignored. Deines says, "They are not always sure their input is important or used in shaping a new direction. The white males do dominate." Deines recognizes these tensions, but does not feel that he has helped directly to improve this situation. He is often asked if the congregations in the black community would be better served by African-American pastors. He responds,

> Everything else being equal, perhaps so, but everything isn't equal. We [the ELCA] do not have an abundance of leaders called to city ministry, nor should African-American pastors be pigeonholed into serving only lower-income and/or African-American congregations. Woman have brought wonderful gifts into the Strategy. We need to continue to be sensitive in including all in the dialogue

and decision-making. I don't think any of this—mutual participation and gift-giving—is as simple as some critics may make it sound. We just keep working at it.

Also inevitable is a level of tension between urban and suburban pastors. Two things have greatly lessened this tension. One is partnerships of city and suburban congregations. The other is Bishop Rogness. According to one lay leader, "Peter has a personality that crosses over so that the suburbanites believe Peter and the people of the city believe Peter. So the tensions between city pastors and suburban pastors are clearly there, but Peter greatly lessens [them]." The important point here is that none of these tensions gets in the way of the ministry of the Milwaukee Strategy in a significant way.

Why It Works

Deines emphasizes that the model is corporate. It is a partnership that includes the three expressions of the church: churchwide (ELCA), synod (Greater Milwaukee) and local (the Strategy). Deines prefers the word "partnership" to the word "corporate." In his words, "I took seriously from the beginning what the ELCA was saying in the coalition model about cooperation, and we work for a real partnership with the national, synodical, and local church. We need all elements working together." Under his leadership, the Milwaukee Coalition has always been active in the national ELCA urban caucus. "We have struggled, in the best sense of that term, constantly with the ELCA in terms of how we can best relate [to] the resources of the ELCA and also trying to share with them what is happening here, because it is a model for the ELCA." The ELCA and the Milwaukee Strategy are entering a deliberate process over the next three or four years, in which the ELCA Division for Outreach would be supportive, interpretive, and collegial in helping the Strategy think out the use of all its resources.

As one example of that cooperation, the Milwaukee Coalition and the ELCA are conducting a two-year experiment. The Strategy has chosen one congregation, which is down to 15 to 20 worshippers but is located in a neighborhood of great need, to use a new approach, Assets Based Community Development (ABCD), to see if they can turn this congregation into a neighborhood outreach ministry. Deines is excited about this new approach:

MICAH works in neighborhoods to pressure employers, governmental officials, and others to improve the quality of life for the poor. ABCD focuses on the assets in the neighborhood to develop the gifts that locale already has. The Milwaukee Strategy will use the ABCD community development model to help rebuild this congregation.

The corporate model includes the financing of this strategy. The Milwaukee Strategy is not self-sufficient. It is and intends to be a partnership that reflects the commitment of the whole church, from the ELCA nationally through the synod, and fundamentally directed at the local level. In order to conduct the ministry it does, the Coalition must develop considerable outside partnership support. One source has been the ELCA through its Division for Outreach. While the ELCA continues to give money for the Milwaukee Strategy and while the Strategy works very closely with the ELCA as to how that money is allotted, the fact is that the amount given has decreased over the past decade. In 1988 funding for Milwaukee Coalition from the ELCA was $147,000, and in 1998 it was $115,000.[20] The amount shows the grant is still considerable but decreasing. What other sources have the city congregations used to develop their budgets?

Partnership Congregations is a program encouraging city churches to form partnerships with suburban congregations for their mutual benefit. Some city congregations have formed partnerships with up to ten or 12 suburban congregations, while others have only one partner. The city pastors think it very important that this be a mutual relationship to avoid the trap, as Jacobson puts it, "where the suburban church is writing checks, and this develops into an implicit superiority."

For example, Jacobson says that the neighborhood minister at his church, who heads up the MICAH core team for Incarnation Church, recently held a neighborhood walk with the alderman and the captain of the city's Fifth District. The walk, he says, revealed sites of "dilapidated houses, busted-up garages, abandoned cars, drug trafficking, and prostitution." Their partner suburban church sent six people on the neighborhood walk with members of Incarnation, and the suburban church has become a member of MICAH. Says Jacobson:

We want to get our core teams together. I like that a lot because the reality of this congregation is that we're strong and fragile at the same time, like a lot of inner-city congregations. But our budgetary realities are not such that we want a lot of financial gifts. I want to keep challenging our membership, whereas for other city churches, [outside financial help] is a matter of survival.

As early as 1991, the Northside Strategy proposed that the synod explore a synodwide funding mechanism for those ministries that "walk with the poor." Bishop Rogness agreed to call together a group to explore that idea, and a team was formed in 1995, resulting in the establishment of the Synod Mission Outreach Fund. The proceeds from the sale of the Augustana Lutheran Church building in Milwaukee for $110,018, together with a grant for $25,000, went to cover administrative costs. This up-front money has ensured that all money raised subsequently will be used for mission ministry projects. Second, the money is designated specifically for Word and Sacrament ministries *among the poor* of Greater Milwaukee Synod.

Congregations are not approached to give money to this fund. Rather, pastors throughout the synod nominate individuals who have great commitment to the church and financial resources so that they usually support many humanitarian causes beyond their own congregations. The bishop, synod staff person, and a pastor or leader in the Milwaukee Strategy informally gather a small number of these people at various homes throughout the synod and share ministry stories from the urban poor with them. In 1998, approximately $65,000 was raised for urban congregations in this fund. And this amount does not include a $200,000 special anniversary gift pledged in 1998 to Peace Lutheran Church by individuals from its suburban partner congregation, Fox Point Lutheran Church.[21]

In early 1997, the Greater Milwaukee Synod took another step by hiring Jeri Jende, a longtime lay volunteer in the Milwaukee Strategy, as resource development director. While her position is still evolving, it has two chief components. One of her tasks is to administer the Outreach Fund. The other part of her position is to raise grant money for the Milwaukee Outreach Training Network. In this latter capacity, during her first year and a half, she has distributed $175,000 in grant money.

Why such a high level of synod support? Jende answers,

[Bishop] Peter Rogness is a key. He is so involved in our Outreach Fund. In fact, along with Dennis Jacobson, he was the primary person involved in getting this started. And right now, as long as his schedule will permit, he goes to every one of the presentations that I set up. He's personally in this; it's his baby. And because he was an urban pastor himself, he definitely knows what that entails and the importance of support both for the pastor as well as financial undergirding. The vision that helps this whole cooperative originates in the bishop.

The corporate model also means that Deines works closely with Bishop Rogness and the Greater Milwaukee Synod. "It has been very easy with Peter as the bishop to have the partnership model. Peter and I haven't disagreed about anything of substance in the years we've worked together." But finally, the Milwaukee Strategy works because the congregations, its leaders, and its pastors are firmly committed to the partnership model. Add to this Deines's deft touch as leader—one who encourages but isn't overbearing. He is one who keeps them to the vision but encourages great variety in how that vision plays out in individual congregations. He is one who finds resources for them and accepts different levels of commitment to the coalition. This cooperative does work. The authors were sent to this site by the ELCA. When we asked the director of urban planning at churchwide offices for a recommendation on which site had the most effective, long-lasting, cooperative urban ministry in the church, this official pointed us to the Milwaukee Strategy, and the authors now know why. We are impressed with the neighborhood ministry in this cooperative.

Future

The pastors and leaders are enthusiastic about the future of this cooperative. In fact, one of their vision documents talks about what ministry will be in place in the year 2025. The only mild reservation we heard expressed concerned the bishop's office. The bishop's term is complete in three years. He cannot stand for re-election, according to that synod's by-laws. Each bishop appoints his or her own staff. If the next bishop has no vision for the city and doesn't want to expend resources there, such an approach could undermine the Strategy. On the other hand, most expect that the next bishop will have a vision for the city, even if that person doesn't have the passion for urban ministry that Peter Rogness does.

But an outsider must raise questions for the future. It is expensive to conduct the Milwaukee Strategy. Most of these congregations do not have large endowments to fall back on. The synod does not have a large endowment for urban ministry either. If giving to national denominations continues to decline, and if the members in these churches continue to be poor, then sometime in the future money could become a defining issue.

The ELCA is committed to staying in the city. Deines says,

> My stance initially is "We will not close any congregations." The neighborhood needs the church, and the church [ELCA] needs the neighborhoods. Rather than use "close" language or merger language—all of which the church has used with these at-risk congregations—we try to identify the direction of outreach needed in this neighborhood and decide how we are going to resource it to make it happen.

In contrast, the Roman Catholic Archdiocese of Milwaukee has consolidated churches in the city twice in the last five years—in 1994 and in 1998.[22]

The Milwaukee Strategy has maintained and encouraged the paradigm of "one pastor, one congregation." Deines argues that there is so much need in a ten- or 12-block radius of an urban church that the need is to focus one pastor and one congregation in one neighborhood. This strategy works in Milwaukee in part because the Lutheran congregations generally are evenly distributed, although on the near Southside and on Wisconsin Avenue, several congregations are very close and serve virtually the same neighborhoods. In this sense of maintaining the "one pastor, one church" paradigm, this strategy is an expensive model of cooperative ministry.

On the other hand, does not the church have a special calling to serve the poor? When neighborhoods become poor ghettos, is it faithful for churches to close or move to the suburbs? In its *Outreach Fund* manual, the Greater Milwaukee Synod enumerates its core values. The church is the Body of Christ embodying Christ's presence in the world. The Great Commission is Christ's mandate to go to *all* people with the Gospel. In terms of attentiveness to the poor, "We understand God's love in Christ is intended for all people, regardless of class; but we also understand Scripture to be abundantly clear that the people of God cease to be faithful when they lose the centrality of care for the poor and forgotten."[23] These core values are the reason the ELCA and the Greater Milwaukee Synod are willing to assist the cooperative so extensively. The approach of Rick Deines is not "How can we save money?" Rather it is, "What is the ministry need?" and then,

"Let's go and find the money." As to why the synod wants to preserve worshipping communities, Pastor Deines says, "We believe it is no longer adequate to simply provide social services to the poor. We must center and anchor our ministries in worshipping communities of faith where people can personally experience God's love and grace."

CHAPTER 5

Mission at the Eastward, Maine

Mission at the Eastward

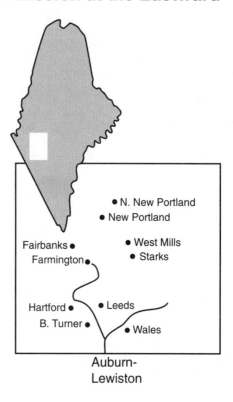

- N. New Portland
- New Portland
- Fairbanks
- West Mills
- Farmington
- Starks
- Hartford
- Leeds
- B. Turner
- Wales

Auburn-
Lewiston

MISSION AT THE EASTWARD

Presbyterian Church in the U.S.A.

Headquarters: Farmington, Maine

Executive Coordinator: The Rev. Scott Planting

Cooperative makeup: nine Presbyterian churches

Birthdate: 1954

Special Ministries: summer camping program,
three housing ministries,youth ministry,
parish nurse council, safe visitors program,
low-income housing corporation, Franklin careers,
and mentoring program

Staff: Executive coordinator, two full-time ordained
ministers, two half-time retired ordained ministers,
one seminary student serving half time, a summer
seminary intern, and a secretary for the cooperative

MATE Chart

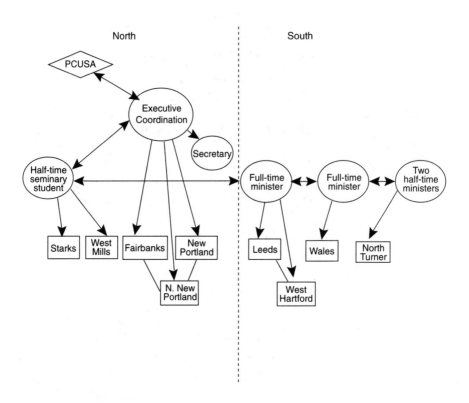

MATECouncil

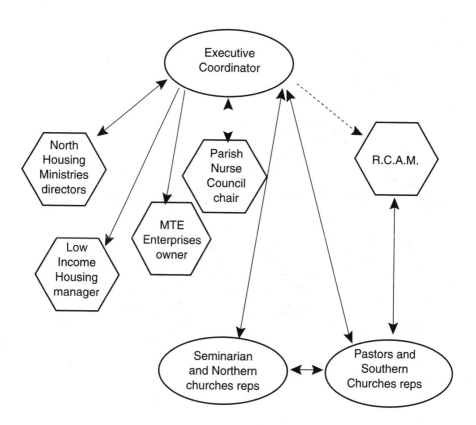

Mission at the Eastward, Maine

W hat distinguishes Mission at the Eastward (MATE) is that it is a mission, and because it is a mission, it has characteristics that are different from a [collection of] congregations." This description comes from Douglas Walrath, treasurer of one of the congregations in MATE. Walrath, who has been involved in MATE since 1981, is a retired professor of rural church studies at Bangor Theological Seminary. He continues, "If you see MATE *primarily* as a cluster of congregations, then you misunderstand it. [MATE contains] some congregations and some ministry points, but we have a whole set of different expectations about the ministry points because MATE's primarily a mission. . . . There are some benefits for the congregations . . . involved in MATE, but [MATE] exists basically for ministry to the communities. This is [its] distinguishing characteristic."

Context

MATE is a cooperative parish ministry consisting of nine Presbyterian churches located in the western portion of Maine, and centrally located on a north-south axis. MATE churches are located in four counties and eight townships. The townships served form two distinct clusters. The southern cluster is made up of the townships of Hartford, Turner, Leeds, and Wales. The northern cluster is made up of the townships of New Portland, Farmington, Industry, and Starks.

The four townships in the southern region are immediately north of the Auburn/Lewiston area, which has one of the larger population masses in Maine—about 64,000 inhabitants. The southern region is about an hour's drive north of Portland, Maine's largest city. Augusta, the state's capital (population 21,325), is 38 miles from Farmington, the largest town in the northern area and the hub of MATE's activities, even though there is no MATE congregation in this college town. The Fairbanks church, three miles outside Farmington, serves the Farmington community. Farmington (population 7,436), located in Franklin County, is the site of one of the several campuses of the University of Maine.

The area of MATE is consistently rural, although the northern cluster is more rural as seen by population statistics. In the north, Farmington, the county seat of Franklin County, is by far the largest with over 7,000 residents, but Industry (population 307), New Portland (765), and Starks (426) are rural. In the south are Hartford (430), Turner (1,415), Leeds (801), and Wales (434).[1]

The areas covered by MATE were thriving areas of Maine throughout most of the 19th century. Fed by the river systems, lumbering and saw mills dominated this area during much of the 19th century and the early part of the 20th. Lumbering was enhanced by an intricate system of narrow-gauge railroads, which ran through many of these small towns.[2] Agriculture was also important during the 19th century. In 1840 Maine ranked second only to New York in bushels of potatoes grown, and the crop averaged about 250 bushels per farm. Kennebec and Somerset counties, which included most of what is now Franklin County, each produced more than a million bushels annually.[3] Both before and after the Civil War, Maine was a beef-producing state and involved in sheep-raising.[4] Even cheese factories developed in this area during the latter part of the 19th century.[5] During the early 20th century, shoe factories also developed. The first Bass moccasin appeared in 1906.[6]

All of these enterprises have declined. Lumbering began to wane in the latter part of the 19th century, and the extensive system of narrow-gauge railroads disappeared in the early part of the 20th century. The advent of the automobile and the development of a highway system bypassed many of these towns. Agriculture was on the decline throughout the 20th century. In 1998 the last dairy farm closed in the upper Sandy River Valley (the Farmington area).[7] Two major shoe factories have closed in the northern portion of MATE in the past 15 years, so that the economy continues to slide. The last Bass shoe factory in this area closed in 1998.

All nine Presbyterian congregations that are now part of MATE are small, reflecting the villages in which they are located. The average attendance in the nine churches is 33 people per Sunday. Only three congregations—Leeds Community Church, Wales Presbyterian Church, and Fairbanks Union Church—have a worship attendance above 50 people per Sunday. Two churches—New Portland Community Church and North New Portland Church—have an average worship attendance of 16 people combined. The remaining churches average 20 to 25 people per Sunday. None of the churches has an average attendance over 80.

Development

The churches of MATE were founded in the 1940s and 1950s in small communities where there was *no* church presence. In other words, the churches of MATE *started* as mission points. At the same time, MATE developed as a mission to the communities and areas in which the churches are located. In fact, community was always a part of these tiny churches. There was no real boundary between church and community. The Presbyterian aspect of this ministry was not emphasized because the word "Presbyterian" had no currency in the area.

Because of the area's economic and social decline during the first half of the 20th century, many of the Methodist churches had closed, leaving several communities without any church presence. The Interdenominational Commission of Maine had requested the help of the Presbyterian Church in the U.S.A. to meet these unchurched needs. Presbyterians were assigned ten unchurched communities.[8] At that time, there was no Presbyterian Church in the U.S.A. presence in Maine.

The first contact of the Presbyterian church in this area of Maine was made in the midst of World War II. Three young men, including the Rev. William Burger, a "lumberjack sky pilot," had gone in 1943 to the area now covered by MATE, where lumbering and farming were the primary industries; he conducted vacation church schools there.[9] By the late 1940s, Bill Burger, by now stated clerk of the Presbytery of Newburyport, visited both Starks and West Mills, providing pastoral care and conducting worship services. Later he participated in the organization of the Presbyterian church in Starks (1949) and West Mills Community Church (1950), and saw that a Presbyterian pastor was assigned to these parishes.[10]

Meanwhile, over a hundred people in Leeds, Maine, had signed a petition requesting help from the Interdenominational Commission in organizing a church in Leeds. The Rev. Carl Geores, fresh from Princeton Seminary, was called in June 1953 to organize the Leeds church and the Hartford parish as a Sunday school missionary. A Sunday school missionary was a minister to areas of scattered populations and provided the services of a pastor there. The assignment was to extend his ministry as quickly and as far as possible.[11] In September 1953, the people in Wales invited Geores to become pastor of the Wales Union Church, which was formally organized the next year.

> The design for the Mission at the Eastward was conceived in a meeting of the General Assembly of the Presbyterian Church in the U.S.A. . . . in Detroit in 1953. . . . It was a well conceived plan to provide a structure through which both human and material resources could be channeled to enable small communities to have living congregations to meet the needs of the people.[12]

The history of MATE has always been connected to the national church. It has not been seen only as a small group up in Maine but also as a mission of the national church. That is, the vision of MATE has always involved the whole church in being part of the life of a cooperative ministry in Maine. Not only did the Presbyterian Church provide money, but also many larger Presbyterian congregations in the Northeast began to visit the churches in MATE and to bring human and financial resources.

By 1954, the Rev. William Burger arrived in Maine and settled in Farmington to serve as the first director of MATE. Burger was an organizational genius, and the coalition, designed at General Assembly, was a hierarchical (top-down) model. The Rev. Carl Geores became associate director. In its history MATE has had one director and two coordinators, all of whom have been committed to a wider community ministry. Burger served as director from 1954 until his retirement in 1973. Geores served as associate director from 1954 to 1973 and as coordinator from 1974 to 1987. The Rev. Scott Planting, the present coordinator, has served in MATE since 1975 and has been executive coordinator since 1987. All three of these men have focused on community development. Scott Planting says, for example, "I see my ministry here—really it's community-development work." To be sure, Planting works community development through the churches.

Therefore, a motif to identify this cooperative is "community development." Not only is community development the emphasis of the present and past directors, but also it is built into the very structure of MATE. The governing council of MATE is made up not only of the churches (pastors and lay representatives) but also of groups, organizations, and social ministries that MATE has helped start but which have a life of their own apart from the churches.

Geores, who has written a history of MATE and the Leeds, Wales, Hartford Parish,[13] calls the years from 1952 to 1962 the decade of organization. These years saw the organization of the Leeds Community Church, the Wales Union Church, the Hartford Community Church, the Fairbanks Union Church, New Portland Church, North New Portland Church, and North Turner Union Church. It also saw the development of the Mission at the Eastward Cooperative and the Camp at the Eastward.[14]

Equally important as the formation of congregations, MATE developed as a way congregations could reach into their communities of considerable crisis and need in the 1950s and 1960s. Under the leadership of Burger and Geores, MATE had the capacity to devise strategies to help congregations engage with their communities around issues of education, housing, and health care. For example, the first medical center in the Leeds area literally grew out of the Leeds congregation, under the leadership of Geores. Likewise, the churches Geores served started to bring tutors to the area to work with students unable to read, and made a push that accelerated the move toward consolidated schools. The tenets of community-building have been used by MATE from the 1960s to the present.

From the beginning there have been two distinct geographical areas where the MATE congregations are located. About half are clustered in the north, where the largest town is Farmington and where Burger lived. Then there is a 40-mile gap to the group of congregations in the south, where Geores lived and where the congregations are much closer to the small cities of Auburn/Lewiston, and only an hour's drive from Portland. The fact that there have always been the two distinct areas has had significant ramifications for MATE.

The decade of the 1960s was a time for testing, experimentation, and expansion of the understanding of MATE. The pastors worked hard to encourage the ministry of the congregations to the low-income people of the area. MATE began three preschool programs and worked on remedial reading. It began a housing ministry that involved building new homes, rebuilding old homes, and making repairs to keep the elderly, single-parent families, and low-income families in their homes. Congregations throughout the Northeast began to send work groups during the summer to work on these housing projects. Many work groups came year after year. These visits have led to close relationships between the pastors and laity of these congregations and MATE. Some retired volunteers have moved to Maine to work in MATE full time, and several young people have become Presbyterian pastors. This housing ministry continues today as a mainstay of MATE.

The building of the Camp at the Eastward became the focus around which a missionwide youth program developed. All the pastors and many laypeople from congregations of MATE were (and are) involved with the camping season by serving as teachers, or as support and maintenance personnel for the campers and facilities. The campers are not only children from the parishes of MATE but also from the communities in which the churches are located. Most of these children have no church home. Scholarships are provided to enable all youth of the area to attend camp. Today, the camp remains the most visible program of MATE to the parishioners in all MATE congregations.

Finally, the 1960s saw MATE begin to work in coalition with government agencies. This partnership with government agencies and other community organizations continued to grow, until today it is often hard to say where the work of MATE and that of a community group begins and ends. This mixture is a product of the rich investment of MATE in the communities over a 30- to 40-year period.

The Rural Community Action Ministry (RCAM) was organized in 1970, through groundwork laid by an ecumenical group of pastors—American Baptist, Congregational, Presbyterian, and Roman Catholic—of Androscoggin, Kennebec, and Oxford counties. Carl Geores spearheaded the effort to form RCAM. (Notice that the northern section of MATE, located primarily in Franklin County, was not a part of this ecumenical group). By-laws were drawn up and approved by the secretary of state for Maine. "The Rural Community Action Ministry was incorporated as a private, ecumenical, nonprofit organization that basically was organized to meet the unmet social needs of the people in the three counties that our organization represented."[15] However, since RCAM involved only the churches in the southern portion of MATE and since what MATE did (and does) and what RCAM did (and does) overlapped, one result was confusion, especially for the people in the southern end. How were the two organizations related, and which was the more important point of cooperative identity for the congregations in the south?

The mid-1970s saw the first major change in leadership. In 1973 Burger retired as director of MATE and pastor of Fairbanks Union Church, New

Portland Community Church, and North New Portland Community Church. Burger's announcement of his forthcoming retirement led to a reorganization of MATE and a two-year period while staff and lay leaders wrestled with a job description for the leader of MATE. In the end, the job description called for a new position: coordinator of MATE. Geores says of the change, "The Mission did not want a Director."[16]

Geores, pastor of the Leeds Community Church, Hartford Community Church, and Wales Presbyterian Church, was elected coordinator of MATE in 1974 and was paid to spend 20 percent of his time in that position. Meanwhile a student at Harvard Divinity School, Scott Planting, arrived as a summer intern in 1974 and served the Fairbanks, New Portland, and North New Portland churches. The parishioners were so impressed with Planting that they asked him to become their pastor. A year later (1975), after graduating from Harvard, Scott Planting was ordained and installed as pastor of these three churches and as a member of the MATE staff.[17]

Planting immediately became a force in MATE, not only as an able pastor to the congregations, but also in expanding ministry in housing, food closets, and work with the United Methodist Economic Ministry. He oversaw the building of a passive-solar house by a coalition of organizations including MATE, the Franklin County Housing Authority, and the (national) United Presbyterian Women's Opportunity Giving. In 1988 Planting (and MATE) worked with the Western Maine Community Action Program, a community action program (CAP) of Franklin County, the Maine State Housing Authority, and the Enterprise Foundation to buy, rehabilitate, and run a low-income trailer park in Farmington. Planting invested himself in community development from the beginning of his ministry. Says Geores, "Over the years Scott has done more to raise the awareness [of] the need for affordable housing for low income people than any other person in Franklin County."[18]

At the end of 1987, after serving almost 35 years in MATE, Carl Geores retired. With his retirement, he tried to put the relationship between MATE and RCAM in perspective: "The Mission at the Eastward and the Rural Community Action Ministry are partners in ministry. The Mission represents the connection to the Presbyterian system of support for the RCAM. The RCAM represents the connection to much of the ministry that goes on in the southern end of the Mission."[19] The complexity of that relationship continues as part of the current story of MATE.

A transition team, formed in 1986, wrote a new job description for the coordinator. Provisions were made for a secretary and a summer seminary intern. Scott Planting was elected executive coordinator of MATE and began his new responsibilities on January 1, 1988. Notice that leadership of MATE has swung from the north under Bill Burger, to the south under Carl Geores and back to the north with the election of Scott Planting.

The present ministers in MATE began their calls soon after Planting's election. He continues as the pastor of Fairbanks Union Church, New Portland Community Church, and North New Portland Community Church, but now spends 20 percent of his time as executive coordinator of MATE. Leeds Community Church and Hartford Community Church called the Rev. Karl Gustafson as their pastor in 1990. Wales Presbyterian Church and Wayne United Methodist Church called the Rev. Kenneth Woodhams as pastor in 1988. Woodhams had been an intern under Planting. In 1997, these two churches decided to drop their yoked situation, and Woodhams chose to remain pastor of the Wales church. Two retired pastors, the Revs. William and Margrethe Brown, served the North Turner Union Church from 1994 to 1998. As they moved into full retirement in September 1998, Scott Planting and MATE were conducting a "visioning process" with the church as to future pastoral leadership. Jeff Scott has served Christ Church, Starks, and West Mills Community Church since 1994. He does this as a tent-making ministry while also working as a home inspector. Jeff Scott, who attended Bangor Theological Seminary, was to graduate in 1999.

Scott Planting reports that if pastors came on board who were not interested in community involvement, it would be tough. Currently, part of the job description for each pastor is commitment to be part of the larger staff. Also, Planting sits on call committees to help guide their process.

Ministries

The distinct missions of MATE illustrate its scope, and also indicate that much of MATE revolves around community-development issues.

1. *North Parish Housing Ministry,* centered in Farmington. This effort encompasses the building of new housing, repair, and rebuilding of existing housing for low-income families. Fourteen or 15 separate Presbyterian churches from all over the Northeast send work groups each summer for one week to work on these houses.

2. *East Parish Housing Ministry*, centered in Starks. This effort is similar to the North Housing Ministry, and ten to 12 separate work groups come to work in the Starks area.

3. *South Parish Housing Ministry*, centered in Leeds. This project is run by RCAM with cooperation by MATE. It hosts 21 work groups during the summer.

4. *The Parish Nurse Council of Western Maine*. This council provides health education, health counseling, referrals to resources, and spiritual support for people living in the area covered by MATE.

5. *Safe Visitors Program*. This effort involves trained volunteers who visit in the homes of isolated people and families at risk and serve as a bridge to resources for them.

6. *Eighty-Two High Street*. MATE manages this 31-unit low-income housing development (at a trailer park in Farmington).

7. *Camp at the Eastward*. A camp run by MATE for the youth of the area, both churched and unchurched. One pastor in the cooperative called the camp the "crown jewel" of MATE. It is certainly the program that is best known in all the churches that make up MATE.

8. *Helping Hand*. This market is similar to a farmer's market except that crafts and other items made by local people are sold, in addition to food.

9. *Franklin Careers and the Mentoring Program*. Scott Planting organized Franklin Careers, which has business people, agencies, and local governmental people sitting around a table together trying to help people make the transition from welfare to work. Currently one of the MATE volunteers has trained 16 mentors to work one-on- one to support these people and help the transition.

10. *Youth Council*. The council gathers the youth from the MATE churches together for areawide events, such as a touring singing group, which has been a hit in all the churches and has built self-esteem among the

youth. Formation of the Youth Council is an outgrowth of Camp at the Eastward.

11. *Summer Intern.* Each summer a seminary student from Princeton (or another seminary) comes to MATE to work with Planting and to experience ministry in this context.

Vision

The MATE organization's central purpose "in the beginning was to set up an administrative system with a budget for Maine ministers with a central treasury and a small mission budget for the work."[20] Since its beginning, MATE has had many different definitions and mission statements. According to former coordinator Geores, "No one definition has ever been completely satisfactory. That is one of its strengths. The mission has always been creative, flexible, and open to change."[21] Most important, from its beginnings MATE has been carrying out the motto of the old Board of Sunday School Mission of the Presbyterian Church, "to reach the last house on the last road."[22]

One layperson said that MATE is a vision that is necessary, just for the vision itself. "I believe that even if MATE just exists as an idea, that it's a vision. Even if all the humans beings that are involved have different perspectives and different ways of handling things or not handling them, that there is value in it, if it just exists on paper, if it just exists in people's minds." MATE is a vision that will not allow its members to be a church closed in on itself. Rather, those who consider seriously what MATE is commit themselves to a mission beyond their own walls to the communities they serve.

Moreover, there is exposure to the church people who come as work groups. Between 45 and 50 outside work groups come to MATE in a typical summer. Their coming exposes MATE's churches to a broader, more inclusive view of the church. As one interviewee put it, "MATE provides a structure for all those churches together to make the circle wider by connecting with the Presbyterian synod and General Assembly. An ecumenical emphasis is advanced when MATE connects with other denominations for work projects."

We began this chapter with Doug Walrath's definition of MATE as a mission, and not simply a coalition of churches. Others in MATE shared their own definitions of this cooperative. One pastor's basic definition of MATE: "It is a cooperative parish of churches [that] have agreed to do common ministry and mission in a geographical area." But he went on to say that it functions primarily for the staff, the pastors themselves, rather than for the parishioners:

> It brings us together and keeps us connected in discussion of all kinds of theological issues. We have serious reflection about theology, serious reflection on Scripture. We wrestle with issues we are facing, and what importance do these issues have to people in our areas and how do we interpret the issues to them.

Another pastor described MATE in terms of a theology of abundance—the multiplication factor in the Body of Christ. In MATE there is an availability of gifts and talents not available in one little congregation. There is an openness and interdependence across MATE that makes the difference. "I know I can call someone in another church who has talents that I don't have in my local parish—a plumber, someone with special biblical or liturgical talents—and that person will respond." This same pastor made this important comment: "Cooperative parish is a state of mind, a way of thinking as well as acting. The question is, 'Do we want to work together?' not 'Will you dance to our agenda?' Cooperatives don't want to project a model on the churches." He added that MATE is a "trust factor enabling people in very small congregations to risk, to innovate, and to become involved in mission. It is a trusting laboratory for people in these congregations."

Even the laity fully involved in MATE found defining it a challenge. For example, Betsy Riley said, "It doesn't get any easier with the length of time here. It's difficult to describe succinctly in a couple of sentences because it is so many different things to so many different people." Her husband, Gil, then offered this definition:

> Fundamentally, it's a cooperative organization, a consortium of rural churches as members that through its staff and resources provides a number of services and programs other than just within the local parish to the ten or so villages in which the churches are located.

He added, "It's that, but that falls far short of describing what MATE is. You have to start talking about individual programs."

Betsy Riley said, "It's a platform in which to be creative in a very nice environment." Because of Planting's leadership, MATE governance is informal, low key, and allows a lot of things to happen. She added:

Scott is willing to try a lot of things, and he doesn't come with all the answers. He comes with the desire to try to see if there is a problem. If so, OK, let's try to figure out what to do about it and then do something about it, without worrying whether or not it is exactly the right thing to do. Let's make some definite progress rather than plan it to death and have it never happen. . . . Scott gives a lot of freedom and encouragement to do a lot of things, and in this environment there [are] always a lot of things that need doing.

When programs grow from a MATE beginning to a broader support basis and MATE can take a back seat, Planting rejoices. The Safe Visitors Program is an example. MATE was the first granting agency, but now this program has been picked up by the Maine Community Foundation. It is connected to MATE, but not all the volunteers are MATE people. Safe Visitors does not carry a MATE banner. Some of the Safe Visitors volunteers know nothing about MATE. This willingness to be only tangentially related to MATE and to the parishioners in the congregations is, as we have seen, something that other pastors have criticized.

Planting's Interpretation of the Vision

In a society that, even in the church world, stresses upward mobility (to larger suburban and urban congregations), Planting has remained as the pastor of three small parishes for 25 years. He says the reason he has stayed so long in one place centers in his understanding of "community." Scott likes poet and farmer Wendell Berry's definition: "Community is a locally understood interdependence of local people, local culture, local economy, and local nature."[23] Planting focuses on the connections in Berry's definition.

For me spirituality means deep inner connection with God and self. But it also means good work, love of the place you live, and contributing to the well-being of your neighbors. Rural ministry takes place in small churches on Sunday mornings, but it also happens drinking coffee in diners, driving in pulp trucks on the way to the mill, visiting the dying in their homes, taking an afternoon brook-fishing with a neighbor.

Planting quotes one of his mentors to express the heart of his ministry:

> A rural pastor I worked with early on gave me good advice: "Do your job and then do what you want to." By that he meant, be a good pastor, preach well, visit the sick, call on the elderly, then discover your heart's delight and pursue it. For me the "do what you want to do" part of parish ministry has been renewal of rural communities, making connections among God and self, work and nature.

Planting elaborates on the theme of community by talking about these villages when they were thriving communities where, he claims, one could literally build a wall around the town and it could almost be sufficient unto itself.

> There was work enough for everyone, small farms produced food, woodlots and small saw and wood-turning mills enough cash to purchase what could be had locally. Neighbors got together to raise barns, and local institutions like church and grange gave a larger frame of meaning to life.

He contrasts yesterday with today:

> Today, in place of practical harmonies are shattering discontinuities. . . . The local economy, once composed of a variety of skilled workers—woodsmen, homemakers, farmers, teachers, millwrights, doctors, blacksmiths—today offers little stable employment opportunity. Schoolchildren are encouraged to seek livelihoods elsewhere, rather than investing their gifts locally. These tears in the fabric of the common life are so apparent in the despair seen on people's faces and reflected in suicide and abuse statistics. The breakdown of local community is a spiritual issue.

Given this situation Planting says there is no more important work for rural churches than the "restoration from the brokenness that is all around us." He argues that community renewal must be accomplished by the community itself from the inside. Instead, most church or governmental agencies think the help will come from the outside in the form of "visiting experts." When the local community gives over what it knows to the "visiting experts," the community is diminished for it. Planting says he has witnessed the loss of confidence in the rural Maine towns. "What has taken me 20 years to understand is that renewal of rural communities begins by practicing what we know. That means learning a local story, even becoming part of that story, and then carefully adding new chapters to the story."

Tensions

MATE is a nationally recognized model for a cooperative. Yet, all cooperatives have structural, personnel, and logistical difficulties. Scott Planting has written, "A cooperative parish holds within it a natural tension between putting energy into the local church and into the cooperative parish. Throughout its history MATE has struggled with this tension."[24] Doug Walrath put it this way: "From all perspectives, cooperatives are an unnatural act. They sound so good on paper, but all you have to do is attend one meeting of a cooperative to realize how unnatural an organization it is." Or as one of the pastors of MATE put it, "MATE is a very inefficient model, and [the pastors of MATE] are very impatient people, each with our own agenda." Finally, a layperson said, "There is a fragile relationship between MATE and the congregation." Surely, such a statement can be made about all cooperatives. In other words, tension is inevitable in a cooperative. We need to examine the visible tensions within MATE to see if they are creative tensions and what is being done to address these tensions.

1. *The tension between the northern section of MATE and the southern section.* Geographically, MATE is situated in two different regions with a 40-mile gap between. Moreover, from the beginning MATE had two strong leaders: Burger in the north and Geores in the south. While the regions combined for joint projects like the camp, each did its own community development for its respective area. In fact, the separation was highlighted when the south organized its social action around RCAM, whereas the north had only MATE. When Burger retired and Scott Planting became a

pastor in the north, Planting worked for community development in the north, while Geores continued his work in the south. These two men worked exceptionally well together. There were so many needs that both of them could especially concentrate in their own geographical area while simultaneously supporting one another. By the time Geores retired in 1987, the economic and social climate had begun to change between MATE's north and south areas.

The urgency of the community-development work in the north remains high, because the economic and social picture has not changed dramatically from the 1950s and 1960s. However, in the south the region's economical environment has improved. The area is becoming more suburbanized as a bedroom community for the Auburn/Lewiston area and even for greater Portland. The southern area of MATE is growing, and so are the churches. The Leeds church, the Hartford Community Church, and the Wales church are all growing, and all of them are now self-supporting. As they grow, according to the pastors, they have more programmatic needs and are more independent and "self-contained." According to one pastor in the south, "There is very little incentive for [these parishes] to be particularly involved in MATE anymore." Moreover, all social services in the south are funneled through RCAM. As Planting puts it, "The mission is humming up here [in the north]. In the south it's pretty much focused in RCAM."

In fact, many of the pastors pointed out that, while RCAM grew out of the life of several congregations, it has become a totally separate, independently funded, independently run agency—a 501(c)(3) nonprofit organization, as defined by the IRS. RCAM's offices are still in the Leeds church, although the organization feels cramped for space and is looking for another office site. The majority of RCAM's board of directors still come from the three churches where Carl Geores had been pastor. Yet the programs are planned and run by staff, with independent funding, and very few parishioners of MATE are directly involved in the work of RCAM. Moreover, the current RCAM staff people are not members of the MATE churches. Planting describes RCAM as "kind of like a mini-CAP agency" (community action program, run by the federal government). Since all the social services work out of that agency, churches have been somewhat free to participate or not. In contrast, in the north, Planting has tried very hard to keep the mission outreach in the life of the church—"sometimes successfully and sometimes not." According to Doug Walrath, Planting understands his position both as a socially active pastor involved in community and as a pastor of congregations, who is there for the members in times of need. Planting brings both of these elements into the worship service. "He tells the people over and over again how wonderful they are as the people of God doing what they're doing."

Because of Planting's stance the congregation in Fairbanks (the largest of the three churches he serves) draws people who want to be involved in community development. "We see ourselves as 'that' flea on the back of this part of the state. It's sort of pressing issues that no one else is dealing with—so we draw people who have either been provided services or who want to be involved in this kind of community ministry."

2. *The Problem of the Visibility of MATE.* Scott Planting is the visible symbol of MATE. He is widely known in the communities where he serves as pastor, among borough, township, and county officials, and among locally based directors of federal programs. He is known by people throughout Franklin County who never attend any of the Presbyterian churches. He is widely known nationally in the Presbyterian Church (U.S.A.) for his pioneering work in MATE. He is an adjunct professor at Bangor Theological Seminary, where he teaches a course a semester, so that he is known by a segment of the theologically trained pastors in Maine.

Do members of the Presbyterian churches in MATE understand MATE as a mission? The not surprising answer is that some do and some don't. Among the churches where Planting is pastor, almost all the parishioners know what he does. They know he ministers far and wide and that provision for his community-development work is written into his call. But harder to estimate is how many members think of themselves as in mission. Douglas Walrath estimates that in the Fairbanks Union Church, half the people think of it as a congregation and are unaware of the scope of the mission.

In the southern portion of MATE, the pastors tell us that a much lower percentage of the members have a thorough understanding of MATE and see MATE as their mission. In fact, one of the pastors serving a church in the southern section claims that only a few of the older, long-term members know what MATE is. Another pastor in the south says, "When I started as pastor several years ago, I would estimate that 20 percent knew of MATE and understood it. Now less than 1 percent of the members understand what MATE is all about." There is a generational change. The generation from the 1950s and 1960s was very involved in MATE, but their children and grandchildren are not. Moreover, the influx of new people into these congregations means that more members have an understanding only of the local congregation.

MATE also suffers from low visibility in the communities where it is most active. MATE is committed, as one layperson put it, "to providing services otherwise unprovided [in these communities]. The pastors provide their services—visit the sick, counsel, marry, bury people, whether church members or not. In this cooperative the pastors and leaders are expected to serve beyond the walls of the church." Another layperson said, "In a small community everyone has a connection with the church in some way." Planting says that one of the reasons the visibility issue exists is that the "clients served are quiet, relatively invisible [people]."

Yet several of the laity wondered how many community people knew anything about MATE. One group of laity from North Portland and North New Portland expressed it this way,

> A sad thing is that many in town do not even know what MATE does, even after Scott's attempted publicity. They do not know from whom they are benefiting. They think that the churches are sustained financially by taxes or some other government/community funds. The people don't ask how it is that the church doors stay open because it may have implications of responsibility.

Occasionally, however, the laity admitted, people in the communities do donate funds or other items for the church's ministry.

In summary, reasons for the low visibility of MATE, especially in the south, are:

- Scott is not their pastor, but is a pastor in the north.
- There is confusion between MATE and RCAM in the southern churches.
- There is a healthier, although not robust, economic climate in the south than in the north.
- New members in the south know little about MATE.
- The majority of MATE projects are in the north rather than in the south.
- Community beneficiaries do not realize that MATE is the reason for the service they are receiving.

3. *Community Development and Congregational Development.* Community development work has been the hallmark of all the heads of MATE. Bill Burger, Carl Geores, and Scott Planting all focused on community development. One of the pastors in the south describes Scott Planting's

work this way: "Scott's a brilliant community organizer. He's one of the best I've ever seen. He is part of that community [Franklin County] in such an integral way that he is able to muster all sorts of energies around all-important agendas."

For 45 years community development has been the stamp of MATE. But the changed circumstances in the southern part of MATE have led some of the pastors to question the current direction of MATE and to push for a transition in the focus of MATE. In fact, the staff and lay leaders describe MATE as a cooperative in transition.

The response about a cooperative in transition was heard especially when we asked interviewees what they would like to see happen in MATE in the next three to five years. One pastor stated that he would like to see more grass-roots programs developed from the people in the congregations. "Scott is a powerful leader type and an exceptional administrator. That is sometimes perceived as a top-down management style which contrasts with the grass-roots piece."

This pastor points to what has happened among the youth who relate to one another through Camp at the Eastward as an example of grass-roots development. The camp experience has brought these young people together from all over the area served by MATE. Beyond the summer experience, the teenagers get together four times a year for retreats. And when they have these retreats, they do mission work together. Recently they have developed an impressive drama and music ministry that they do throughout the territory of MATE. The youth are even talking about taking their drama and music ministry to some of the "work group" churches throughout the northeast. While they are together, according to one of the pastors, "these kids do a lot of theological reflection, when they are sitting around at camp, and when they are on retreat. These kids are savvy in their faith." What is even more surprising is that development of the youth program has required very little energy from the staff of MATE. It has been driven by the young people and their energy and by the community that is formed around the camp. Scott Planting says it's one of the most significant things he's seen in 25 years in terms of a program that has taken off from the grass roots.

Scott Planting acknowledges the need for more programs bubbling up from the congregations themselves. "We were organized as a top-down model. Now we're trying to reverse that a little bit and ask, 'How can communities take hold of their own lives?' and then we can provide resources for what *they* want to do."

However, one pastor suggests that a lot of what is now happening in MATE does not come out of the congregations but is really the work of the coordinator and his vision and connections. How involved are the parishioners in much of the community-development work? He suggests that, except for the camp, lay involvement is almost nil, at least in the southern portion of MATE. Yes, he says, "the programs are MATE-connected or affiliated but don't involve many people from the churches."

One layperson described Scott as "the greatest community organizer I've ever seen." Scott's view of his own leadership issue is this: "The leadership issue becomes how much do I as a person have a vision and try to pull people to share that vision, or do I just wait for something to bubble up."

Why It Works

1. Understanding Rural Culture

Douglas Walrath has written extensively about the difference between rural areas and metropolitan and suburban areas.[25] One of his complaints is that denominational officials try to turn rural churches into suburban churches, thereby alienating the long-term rural people. If there are enough "suburbanites" moving into a rural area, they change the rural church to look like a suburban church in a town-and-country setting. The locals either leave the church entirely or else cede the leadership positions to the often better-educated and more articulate suburbanites. It takes a different kind of approach to minister effectively among rural people.

In our interview, Walrath used the image of lawns.

> You can tell almost everything about the kind of ministry and culture that is suitable for a congregation by the way in which people deal with their lawns. In rural areas, people don't plant the lawn. We mow whatever comes up. In suburban areas, you plant a lawn and try to keep the lawn in a certain way—kill the crabgrass, get the dandelion, and so on. Here if we pull the weeds, we wouldn't have any lawn.

Planting's genius, according to Walrath, is that he understands that to have a long-term ministry here you have to deal with what comes up. "Scott is able to deal with the staff that is given to him; he deals with the attitudes in congregations that are there. He can deal with the amount of money that is there. He can deal with the organizational realities that are presented to him. In short, he is able to adjust his ministry to the actual situation."

Doug Walrath finds Scott Planting's approach to be a compelling theological model. "Jesus called the 12 disciples, and after that he is stuck with them. He never tries to change the organization by recruiting a different 12. He worked with what he had. Jesus recognized that whatever ministry is going to happen is going to have to come out of this group." Walrath's approval of this model is shown by his next comment: "I think this is a more relational and spiritually sound model of church than the organizational model of church which is most popular right now."

2. Empowering People

Empowerment is important to the leaders of MATE, and this means emphasizing and developing local leadership. Under Scott Planting's leadership, MATE was instrumental in starting a computer components manufacturing firm, Manufacturing and Technical Enterprises, Inc. [MTE], 15 years ago to provide employment for displaced shoe-industry workers. Alison Hagerstrom, a member of the Fairbanks church today, had been executive secretary to a mill owner for many years. Scott Planting recognized that after ten years as the owner's secretary, she could do her boss's job. Therefore, Scott asked her to be manager of this new firm. MTE was purchased by its president, Alison Hagerstrom, in 1993. In June 1998 the MTE plant burned to the ground. This event threatened the future of MTE, but through the efforts of Hagerstrom and advice from Scott Planting and others, the company has survived this disaster and continues to provide needed employment for the area. Today Hagerstrom chairs the Maine governor's statewide small-business committee. On one of the days the authors were interviewing at MATE, the governor was visiting the plant. Says Hagerstrom, "Scott thinks you can do things that you don't think you can do."

Elena Barker, also a member of the Fairbanks church, has been manager of the 31-unit low-income housing project at 82 High Street, Farmington, for ten years. When she applied for the job and was asked her qualifications, she said she was the mother of eight children and also the Franklin County bond commissioner. While she had never managed any kind of business, she was hired and has made the housing project work.

On a smaller scale, MATE offers opportunities beyond what a small rural congregation might to anyone who is interested and willing to work. Says one retiree: "MATE offers challenge and fellowship I haven't found in other places since I retired from teaching. It offers volunteer opportunities for older, retired folk." About Planting's influence on this empowerment, she adds, "Scott has a way of getting people to do things on their own." Says another layperson, "You don't usually have to ask more than once if there's something you want to do." Says Planting, "Laypeople have been raised up and empowered when they take leadership positions. The most exciting thing I've seen in my ministry here is just that!"

3. Use of Full-time Volunteers

Scott Planting says, "We have a growing number of full-time volunteers in mission. These are mostly early-retirement people who are quite skilled and come up here (to rural Maine as part of MATE) to work for a short time but who stay on. They bring incredible resources." Gil and Betsy Riley are prime examples of such volunteers.

For five years the Rileys were part of the work group that came to the North Parish Housing Project from the Presbyterian Church, Wilton, Connecticut. When this couple took early retirement in 1991, the Rileys had been so touched by the work of MATE that they decided to move to Maine for two years and volunteer until they were ready for full retirement. In those two years they became so involved in the work of MATE that they knew they did not want to leave. They have bought a retirement home near Farmington and plan to stay as long as their health holds.

In the final year before her retirement Betsy Riley had been manager of an abused-women's center in Connecticut and headed the Senior Volunteer Program, matching volunteer work with older people willing to do the work. This employment turned out to be excellent training for programs she would start in MATE. Finding no abused-women's center around Farmington, Riley became a volunteer for SAFE, a sexual-abuse emergency hot line. She has continued on this hot line for seven years.

In connection with the Community Action Program, which distributes the federally funded programs of aid to the poor, Betsy Riley began to visit isolated families and individuals with "heavy-duty" issues and struggles. In doing so, she conceived the idea of Safe Visitors. She would train others to be safe visitors, taking the philosophy of creating a safe place for people to discuss and plan changing their lives.

Betsy Riley went to Scott Planting and said, "If we could get an umbrella grant—we don't need much money—we could make this work. I'd like insurance to cover the volunteers and money to have a professional [who will] brainstorm with us once a month over the issues we face." So Planting obtained a $3,000 initial grant from the Northern New England Presbytery, and Safe Visitors was born. Seven years later, Betsy oversees 50 visitors. They visit with needy families in the area, usually on a weekly basis.

In turn, Safe Visitors has led to seven of the visitors being trained as hospice volunteers and also to young volunteers who work in teams and take children out for safe playtime. Riley has created networks with women's mission groups in Presbyterian churches in the Northeast to send gifts for families and newborn babies, crafts, projects, etc.

Betsy Riley is also coordinator of MATE's Parish Nurse Program. The program has four paid part-time people. Three are registered nurses, one of whom is a holistic nurse; the fourth writes grants and works behind the scenes. These nurses go into the homes of people with health issues who are falling through the cracks of federally funded health systems, seeking any resources that might help.

In connection with Franklin Careers, which Scott Planting started, Betsy Riley works with a mentoring program for people trying to go back to work from welfare. The economy is very thin in this part of Maine. With the few jobs that are available, many of the people are not ready to go to work. Her job is to get the community actively involved in supporting the would-be workers one on one. Currently, she has 16 trained workers. Says Riley: "A healthy person from the community is connected with an isolated person to try to build bridges."

When Gil Riley retired, he came to MATE with a particular responsibility. He became director of the North Parish Housing Ministry in 1991. He said, "Very quickly I learned that poor housing was only one piece of the puzzle." Poor housing was often interrelated with health issues, educational issues, and cultural issues. Gil Riley's work started to have many interconnections with the kind of work his wife was doing.

As director of the housing ministry, Gil Riley's busiest season occurs between mid-June and mid-August each summer when work groups come from various Presbyterian churches in the Northeast. In the "off-season" and because of the interconnectedness of issues, he began to develop networks with other agencies, and especially the Western Maine Community Action Program, a CAP program headquartered in East Wilton, Maine (close to Farmington). As these networks began to develop, the hard boundaries between housing needs and other needs began to soften.

Riley became interested in what he could do to help on the economic-development end, which coincided with Scott Planting's interest in economic development. Thus, Riley became involved in economic-development issues that are officially unrelated to MATE. Planting and Riley share a fundamental philosophy: "If you are trying to help people, it doesn't matter what the agency is!" Gil Riley helped in the start of the community market. Says Riley: "Anything to develop a few more bucks for people who need more bucks to live on." He also helps in a financial advisory capacity with MATE.

Betsy and Gil Riley talked about their decision to "retire" to work for MATE and other community-development issues. Said one: "People think we are nuts. They ask, 'Are there real people up there?—someone you can talk to? You mean you still like it?'" The Rileys have such a deep level of satisfaction with their lives that they have helped persuade four other retired couples to work in MATE for the entire summer and one couple to volunteer year-round. "We could never go back to the corporate world and the lifestyle we left behind [in a suburban community outside New York City]." In fact as one of the authors interviewed them, Betsy Riley tried to persuade him to take early retirement and move to Maine to help in the community-development projects. "Why would anyone want to retire and play golf every day?"

4. MATE's Commitment to Struggling Congregations

Scott Planting worries about the smaller, struggling congregations within MATE. He believes the smallest churches like Starks, West Mills, and the New Portlands are places where there is a critical need for the church. Not only are the congregations struggling; the towns are likewise in decline. Planting points out that these churches reflect their communities. They're always mirror images of one another. The same dynamics that go on in the life of these churches is reflected in the community. Therefore, says Planting, "these churches have a tremendous ministry to these communities. Our children by and large leave. There is very little for children. The economic basis of these places is incredibly vulnerable. So, having a worshipping community that will be sustainable is very, very important to MATE. In the small churches, like New Portland, where we had 18 people yesterday, the prayer lists are so long, from people who have lost jobs, mill closings, cancer, family issues. I'm content that we just lift up these people in prayer week after week. We even get to visit some of them, some of the time." Planting emphasizes that one of his long-term goals is to keep these places going. Sadly, he adds, the denomination finds almost no reason to keep these churches open. "Why would you keep churches with less than 25 members in dying communities going?"

When another pastor was asked what he would like to see in MATE, he pointed to the continuance of the congregations themselves.

> It's real simple. All of us staff have a real commitment to these congregations and viability of ministry that these small churches have in these communities, different as they are from one another. I would hate to see our various congregations die. Whatever we can do to help them keep going—whether it's financial, moral support, or whatever—that's what we need to be about. . . . Social ministry needs to be coming out of these congregations, and if we don't keep these congregations alive, then there is no point in community-development work. My focus is to support these congregations and let the rest of it flow from this base.

All the pastors in MATE agree with this principle. All of them want to help keep the struggling churches open, because often only one church is still open in the community. In fact, all the pastors agree that MATE needs to find better ways to fund service for individual struggling congregations. Planting says, "My sense of MATE is that we provide a regional identity. We also provide some service to individual congregations, and we could do a better job with that."

5. MATE's Commitment to Its Communities

There is not an absolute line between MATE's commitment to its struggling congregations and its commitment to the communities in which they reside.

The social-ministry focus of MATE is aimed at needy community members rather than church members (unless they are the needy). All the pastors consider the communities in which they serve to be their parish since there is no other church presence there. The pastors visit, counsel, and bury community members as well as church members. One member of the North Turner church put it this way: "People who are involved know the importance of MATE for North Turner to survive. But others in the community and those peripherally involved, who expect the church to be present in the community to hatch, match, and dispatch its people, do not know about MATE. These folk are dedicated to the longevity of the community church, sustaining it, but they are not connected to its source of sustenance—MATE." Nevertheless, it is because MATE is a missionary force in these communities that MATE receives churchwide funding.

6. Commitment of Pastors to Each Other

Margrethe Brown said simply, "For us as pastors [MATE] has been a unique community of caring and concerned pastors. The biggest impact on us has been good colleagues in ministry with whom you work. It has been a delightful experience." One report which we heard consistently from the pastors was that the present group of clergy were committed to one another and to their mutual ministry. The pastoral staff meets every other week for almost a half-day. They begin with prayer and Bible study, do some lectionary study for the Sundays coming up, conduct business, and serve as support for one another. In this setting all clergy say they can be and are totally honest with one another, and that they attack theological and societal issues in depth.

Karl Gustafson emphasized "connectedness":

All the pastors have commitment at least to the concept of cooperative ministry. We view church and ministry as a corporate, connected whole and not just isolated little pieces doing isolated little things. This is part of our common theological conviction, spiritual conviction, and ideological conviction. All of us have the concept of "connectedness." All of us are committed to a vision of the church which says we're all in this together and we need to find ways to be a community together.

Ken Woodhams said that in parish ministry clergy often do not want to work together because of turf issues.

> To do cooperative ministry means that your own ego has to get out of the way. You're not in this to put on your resume, "I've grown a church from zero to 1500 and increased the budget a hundred-fold and done all this." What has to be the focus of the staff is "How can the church in this place best be served as a living, growing entity and what can we do to help that?" We have to be like gardeners planting the seeds rather than harvesters boasting about what we've done, when it's really the work of the people and our part is to empower them to do their work.

Jeff Scott said that as a temporary supply pastor at Starks/West Mills since 1994 he feels that he is never alone. "There is this wonderful support network. It is an umbrella or connectional system that opens one up to all kinds of relationships and responsibilities . . . You won't burn out because you don't feel alone, which often happens out in the 'boondocks.' You get stale, burned out, and become disengaged." At another point in the interview, Jeff Scott said, "Cooperatives do have to be a very intentional thing. You have to be committed to it, invested in it, and willing to spend the time and effort to make it work."

Planting himself says that the pastors form a very strong group, and that he would not have stayed for 24 years without the support of the staff. "I see the other ministers who work pretty much by themselves out here. They die! They have difficult parishes; they have no resources; they're all by themselves. They deal with these incredibly dysfunctional systems. And they die. Often they end up hating small churches or small communities, and they're so shattered. We are a very good support system for one another."

7. Planting as Leader

One layperson described Planting this way:

> He likes working in collaboration with other clergy. He is not their boss, as he is a pastoral colleague with his own charges. He is

intelligent, good with people, sensitive to feelings and situations, and has a good sense of humor. He is very good at bringing things about. He is persuasive, but not with a dictatorial style. He may adopt a confrontative style, dealing with what is before MATE. However, he is a good listener, in spite of his busy schedule.

Another layperson said:

These cooperative parishes in a rural area, from my perspective, function on personalities and the willingness of persons to make the necessary connections. They do not function on a hierarchical governance and, even though Scott Planting is the coordinator of MATE, he cannot—even if he desired—run MATE. It's bigger than its parts. It only functions because of its individual parts working together, hence, the cooperative.

Therefore, this interviewee used the analogy of Body of Christ (1 Cor. 12) as the best image for MATE.

Doug Walrath reports that Planting could choose to do a lot of community-development work on his own with the contacts he has, but he always works to make community-development projects a part of MATE. Planting has many ideas and tremendous energy. Said one of the pastors of MATE, "Scott has a lot of 'I have a dream' speeches."

Jeff Scott summarized it well:

Sometimes there is resistance to Scott [Planting] charging ahead with his grand visions. Scott will say, "I've talked to so-and-so and this is our plan." Something will be under the guise of MATE, but it will really be just a wonderful entrepreneurial thing that Scott's developed with somebody else. Some will complain, "That's not a MATE plan; that's a MATE label on something not directly related to the churches."

On the other hand, Jeff Scott immediately added, "Scott is open and tries to invite people to be involved. People may have some initial resistance. 'I'm not really interested.' And then when it evolves in a great program, the pastors will complain, 'Hey, you didn't involve me in this.'"

MATE works because all the pastors are committed to the cooperative, although they argue about its form. Moreover, their relationships with one another are such that they can be completely frank and honest with one another when they disagree. Planting said of one of the other pastors, "We're like brothers. We love one another, but we fight a lot." MATE works because Planting is able to work with what is presented to him—situations in the communities, the pastors called to the churches, and the people who are members of the parishes. MATE also works because he searches for outside resources. As he puts it, "Often ministers only look to the church for resources. There is a world of resources outside the church."

8. Outside Work Groups

MATE also works because of the outside groups that come to work each summer. The members of MATE, the people in the communities served by MATE, and the work-group volunteers—all benefit from the Work Group program. The primary purpose of the work groups is to help economically deprived residents benefit by having work done at their residences, including the construction of entire homes. But the side benefit, equally important to the authors, is what happens to the members of the MATE churches and to the work-group members.

Said Jeff Scott: "Outside work groups come and really energize you. They worship with you and they share their stories of God's grace with you. It energizes our people and develops a willingness to meet the outsider." Just as important is the way the whole program benefits the work-group members. Scott Planting says that as the work groups complete their week of working on the housing needs, there is always a banquet and communion service on Friday night attended by the work group, members of the MATE churches, and the people who have been helped. "We create a new community of people from 'away' and local people. And this service is a very powerful, unforgettable experience for people to go through. We give a heart back to an awful lot of people."

The authors asked the Rev. Karin Carroll, pastor of Camp Hill Presbyterian Church, a suburb of Harrisburg, Pennsylvania, to describe what Camp Hill's work group does and the effect on the congregation. This church has completed its 13th trip to MATE, going every year since 1986. According to Pastor Carroll, the congregation sets a limit of 40 people who can go on the trip, which matches well with MATE's limit of 35. Three of the volunteers do nothing but take care of the cooking and meal cleanup for their people. A fourth person, the crew coordinator, is not on any individual crew but travels around to all the crews, making sure each has the materials needed. Finally, a fifth person, the pastor, is not a full-time worker because she is arranging all the devotions and preparing for the final dinner and communion service. The work group stays at a University of Maine-Farmington dormitory and members eat all meals at Old South Congregational (UCC) Church in Farmington. Last year the Camp Hill team brought seven vans to haul the workers, equipment, and materials for their work.

"The work we do," said Carroll,

> is housing rehabilitation work. . . . We take shacks, trailers, other existing buildings, some of which have been damaged by fire, or are in a state of dilapidation. We rehabilitate them; sometimes we [build] on an addition, often we reroof a building, we put in ramps for people with disabilities, and we do a lot of scraping and painting. . . . We have helped to rehabilitate a whole trailer park [82 High Street] and put in playground equipment there.

Pastor Carroll praised MATE as an exceedingly good volunteer organization.

> To be able to take volunteers as they come into town for a week, many of whom are unskilled, and have them be fully employed doing things that actually help build something is not that easy. I've been involved with many volunteer groups, including the Peace Corps, and I've seen how difficult it is to do this. A lot of my fellow Peace Corps volunteers went home because they didn't have jobs that materialized. The groundwork had not been done well enough. MATE is one of the best-run volunteer efforts I have ever seen in my life. . . . It is a year-round mission, and that means that the infrastructure is there identifying people and choosing the projects with an eye to unskilled volunteer help. And there are professional construction people—carpenters, masons, and other professionals—to supervise the work. These professionals are extraordinary teachers and mentors.

Karin Carroll says that these visits have a huge impact on the congregation in three areas. *First, the visits help approach the issue of the U.S.*

economy at a systemic level. The impact is first on the people who go as mission volunteers, but it spreads to the congregation.

> When you begin to work with the working poor, it raises the systemic question, "Why?" You can help rehabilitate houses for people who have undergone tragic situations, like their house has burned down, or debilitating illnesses, and say that is what we are meant to do. But here you work on the house where this man is the breadwinner with a good job by Maine standards, a supervisory job at a shoe factory, and he is earning between $12,000 and $13,000 a year. They have only one mattress in the entire house, where husband and wife sleep while the kids sleep on piles of clothes, and there is no running water in the house and the stench is terrible. The home is basically a two-story shack. Then you begin to ask the question, "Why?" You ask the corporate question about the economic system and not about the individual. Why in this country do we have a system which cannot provide a job with living wages for people, so they can have just the basics of a decent place to live?

This exposure enables us in the church to begin to ask questions about the system of which we are all a part, questions that are hard to raise in church because they are seen as "political." Says Carroll,

> The American dream that everyone who works hard can have all the basics of a good life is not always true in south-central Maine. The entire economy is poverty-stricken; the entire place is without resources. This is the question we bring back to the congregation. When some people say, 'These people are poor because they will not work,' we say, 'Beg your pardon, but we know someplace where that's not true. It's the system which needs a lot of fixing, and the system which is sinful.'

Second, MATE helps deal with the issue of faraway missions as opposed to local missions. Carroll has found today a much greater reluctance than in past years to donating money to faraway missions. The constant refrain is, "Let's do something to help the people around here. Let's do something in our own neighborhood." The visits to Maine show the need for missions far away. The work groups convey the message that faraway missions have great need and do great good. To show what has been done, in the fall, the Camp Hill congregation always has a victory dinner with pictures, videotapes, and slides to show people what has been done with the money they contributed. Thus, the work groups help develop the *connectional church*.

The trip costs the Camp Hill church between $10,000 and $11,000 a year. The church asks for extra offerings for this project. A few in the congregation give little or nothing and say, "Why aren't you doing something closer to home? Why not do more in Harrisburg?" Says Carroll: "We have a twofold answer to that. One is that we indeed are involved in Harrisburg. We also have a $10,000 to $11,000 project in Harrisburg as well. . . . But Harrisburg has all kinds of resources. It has wealthy people, large corporations, people with all kinds of incredible skills. If it wants to do something about a problem, it can put all its resources together and begin to tackle the problem. MATE covers a section in south-central Maine that does not have these resources. So the help has to come from the outside."

As a result of the years of sending work groups, the Farmington area has become a home away from home, a church away from church, for a lot of church members. According to Karin Carroll, "As more and more of the congregation has gone on this trip and as we've brought Scott Planting back to preach here, we strengthen these ties. We get across the importance of the MATE project, and this project opens it up so that we can get it across for other distant missions."

A third benefit is the self-esteem and sense of the church that is developed in teenagers by making this trip. Pastor Carroll says,

> It's a great thing for males because it is a construction thing. It's also a liberating thing for a number of females—teenagers and adults—that they can do these things. This year for the first time we had a female crew leader! These youth feel no lack of confidence in taking out a hammer and tackling a roof or a dry wall. This is not a youth trip. We do not cater to the youth, and paradoxically it is one of the reasons they want to come.
>
> It also teaches them about the corporate church. They think they can be perfectly fine Christians without the church. The institutional church is "yuck." After they go on the MATE trip, they realize that there is no possibility that this can be done as an individual. It

requires enormous institutional investment year around at the Maine side of it. And it requires an enormous institutional investment by the church that is going. It has been a real blessing to my two teenagers and to all the others who have gone.

Future

1. Finances

MATE has lived on subsidies since its beginning in 1954. Because the Presbyterian Church sees MATE as a mission, it has been willing to subsidize the endeavor. As the authors worked with the cooperative, we learned that MATE has been told that subsidies will be greatly reduced or even eliminated by the year 2000. Is this good news or bad news?

When asked what most threatened the future of MATE, the most common answer was finances. One lay member said, "Money—it takes finances to keep providing service. That's a sad thing to say, isn't it?" Another answered, "Financial difficulties—MATE's dependency on [the] synod in this regard." Another expressed this wish, "It would be nice if all the churches were comfortable, not struggling."

Congregational self-sufficiency is the goal for the larger of these small churches. In fact, two of the MATE churches have become financially self-sufficient in the last few years. One lay member said that he sees "this as the primary, yet unattainable goal of MATE—to provide the needed resources to make each congregation self-sufficient."

Even a cursory examination of MATE reveals that some of the smallest churches, located in tiny, dying communities, will not be self-sufficient soon. What should be done with these struggling congregations? One option, sound from a financial viewpoint, is to close these churches. However, some are the sole churches in their communities; also there are no other community centers. The authors, along with the ministers and leaders of MATE, argue that these congregations ought to remain open for the service they provide to the communities.

Scott Planting's approach to financing for the future of MATE seeks to offer a sharing of resources among equals. Scott proposes to invite formally the affluent churches that make up the work groups to put an item in their yearly budget for MATE. Such a budget item would be an outright gift to MATE, in addition to the cost of sending a work group to Maine. (Costs for sending a work group to help in MATE are borne by the work-group congregations.) Planting argues that this arrangement is a fair balance because MATE gives as much back to the work-group churches as MATE receives from the churches.

Without MATE at least four of the congregations would close. The others would survive as small isolated congregations struggling to pay their pastor. Most of these remaining congregations would find some yoking arrangement to ensure the presence of a paid ordained leader. Each congregation would be much more likely to turn in upon itself, and the pastors would feel more isolated and lost, as Planting has suggested.

Finally and most significantly, Planting himself says that he does "not worry about the finances that much because when you have interesting, helpful programs going on, *the money follows*." Moreover, Planting teaches nonprofits to break even financially for the services they provide "so they don't just rely on grants." He is convinced that as long as the mission to these communities flourishes, money will be found to conduct the ministries.

2. Mission and Evangelism

MATE is to be greatly admired for its mission to serve the communities where the churches are located. Does this service orientation bring people to worship? Do the pastors of MATE emphasize evangelism as much as they do service? It must be stated that Scott Planting's understanding of the church puts serving the community before trying to attract people to attend the churches of MATE. Nevertheless, there is modest growth in at least four of the churches. Fairbanks, the largest of the small congregations where Planting serves as pastor, is growing. Specifically, the church attracts people who have a servant mentality like Planting's and people who have been helped by MATE. Since Jeff Scott assumed the pastoral leadership of Starks and West Mills, the two churches, which had almost died and had fewer than ten in attendance, have begun to blossom and grow and now average from 25 to 35 people per Sunday. The use of a rock band at Starks has attracted people under age 35 and many children. The Starks-West Mills congregations are heavily dependent on MATE and would have closed long ago except for MATE. The Leeds congregation under Karl Gustafson and the Wales congregation under Ken Woodhams—both located in areas of modest population growth—have grown in recent years.

One layperson talked about the need for a greater evangelism thrust. Significantly, she lives in the southern region of MATE, where there is population growth, not in the northern portion where many communities are declining. She says that not enough is being done to make worship the center of growth. Making a distinction between social-service activities and church building activities, she criticizes MATE, saying that the mission has too much of the former and not enough of the latter. "We're right at a crucial space where more outreach about the faith needs to be done, in bringing people to Jesus Christ. And I don't think that that's a focus [of MATE]." She continues that it could be a major focus, that people do talk about bringing more people into the churches, but no action is taken. She feels that the congregations themselves are stuck at the status quo, with no mission or purpose (for bringing people to a saving relationship to Jesus Christ through the church). "I don't think that it's as explicitly stated as it might be that MATE is a church organization. The pastors aren't making theological connections to their social ministries." Therefore, she wants MATE to focus more on worship and faith-centered decision-making.

3. Scott Planting

Because Planting is such an excellent, committed, and faithful leader of MATE, one layperson said that his very competence raises questions about how MATE will change when he leaves. She argued that Planting is so good and so committed to what he does that he has gained a lot of tacit authority not only in MATE but also in Franklin County. "Sometime in the future Planting will leave [or retire] and take that authority with him. Either the laity and clergy left there will rise to the occasion, or MATE will remain in name only with no power."

The leaders of MATE look with confidence to the future. They are convinced that as long as MATE serves a vital ministry to the communities where it is located, the cooperative will thrive. Planting is the third-generation leader of MATE, and most of his colleagues are convinced that there will be a fourth outstanding leader. Cooperatives change, so it is possible that sometime in the future one or two of the churches in the southern portion of MATE will pull out to go on their own. But all the ingredients discussed above regarding "why MATE works" mean that these changes will not be immediate. Scott Planting is not inordinately concerned about finances for the future, believing, as we do, that when the mission is served, the money will come.

CHAPTER 6

Conclusion: Key Features of Cooperative Ministry

Conclusion:
Key Features of Cooperative Ministry

O ut of the stories of cooperatives that we have studied, we can now make a number of generalizations about key features of coopera tive ministry. We offer these now as lessons for those who might be thinking of experimenting with congregational cooperation in their own context. We offer them also as further portrayals of the nature of American congregations in the late 20th century.

1.   A Viable Mission Posture

Cooperatives create a credible mission posture for congregations of tradi-tional denominations that face the challenging circumstances of the North American environment. What Douglas Walrath said about MATE, we can say about all five cooperatives: "What distinguishes [it] is that it is a mission, and because it is a mission, it has characteristics that are different from [a collection of] congregations." In all five cases in this book, the cooperative strategy has moved individual congregations beyond the struggle for institu-tional survival. The congregations involved have been turned outward in their foci. Community needs in a local mission area have a platform and a hearing within a cooperative parish arrangement. Cooperation mitigates the tendency to self-absorption that seems to be systemically present in Ameri-can congregational life. The omnipresent issues of institutional maintenance shrink into a larger set of issues defined more by the mission of the whole church than by the success of atomized organizations. To be sure, the three older, more mature cooperatives—USMP, MATE, and Milwaukee—exhib-ited mission to outsiders more fully than did the very young cooperatives—

North Central and Tri-County. Nevertheless, however the cooperatives define it, mission is the central focus.

Perhaps most ingenious in the cooperative style of mission is its accommodation of a legitimate degree of local ownership for individual congregations. In this regard cooperatives exploit the paradoxical power of disestablishment in American religion. The American environment militates against hierarchy and centralization. It promotes high levels of lay ownership, participation, and commitment on the part of a wide segment of members. Insofar as cooperatives balance individualism and association in their structures, they advance a grand American tradition in church life. Their posture, in turn, is identifiable with the historic Christian sense of mission as active witness and service. Cooperatives have stemmed the devolution of congregational life into inert self-selected interest groups.

2. Empowerment for Lay Ministry

The Cooperative Parish strategy empowers people and releases lay ministry. In the five cooperative parishes studied, we observed laypeople catching the vision of the cooperative and then taking charge of critical aspects of the mission of that cooperative. As one layperson put it, "For some people, the parish has expanded their notion of what it means to be the church." The well-worn patterns of codependency between laity and clergy, especially laity expecting clergy to be their personal chaplains, were conspicuously absent or muted in the cooperatives we visited. Beyond the initial aches and pains of adjusting to change, lay attitudes ranged from satisfaction to real enthusiasm for the vigorous mission of the cooperative. Members felt that they belonged to a healthy part of the church and were participating in worthwhile mission.

In cooperatives, laity are empowered and given a structure in which to minister to others. In the coalitions we studied, clergy were resource people. In fact, clergy, judicatory officials, and bishops exhibited partnerships with laity in the parishes we studied. Professionals in the church were welcomed for their critical perspectives as often as for their access to denominational purse strings. The restructuring of congregational ministry within cooperatives released the energies of members in Maine, West Virginia, Alabama, North Dakota, and Wisconsin.

The "baptismal ministry of every member" that Bishop John Smith treasured was gaining elbowroom through cooperative parishes. Bishop Smith wrote, "The reality of the baptismal ministry of every baptized person, sharing in mutual covenant with one another, lies at the heart of Cluster Ministry. . . . What is at stake is the recovery of a vision of ministry of the whole people of God in which ministries of all baptized members are integrated with one another."[1] We agree. The "priesthood of all believers" is being lived out in extraordinary ways in these cooperatives.

We acknowledge that not all members of the cooperatives have caught this vision. Many simply come to church and do not become involved in the mission. But, this fact of noninvolvement is true today, and always has been true, of Christian congregations. Even the largest and fastest-growing megachurches in this country—churches like Willow Creek Community Church near Chicago—report attendance at their seeker services to be more than three times greater than participation by active members who carry out the ministry. What is distinctive about cooperatives is that they provide a structure that invites people to become involved.

3. Community Service and Development Ministries

Cooperative parishes have proved themselves to be effective at generating and supporting community service and community development ministries. In many ways cooperative parishes are an ideal structure for community service and development. Cooperatives provide a bird's-eye perspective on community needs that would otherwise escape the notice of isolated congregations, and a cooperative community can define area needs more effectively than individuals, congregations, or even community services in some cases. The cooperatives in this book gave birth to community services in critical cases of unmet needs. In this capacity a cooperative gives congregations a greater and more effective community presence than they would have had otherwise. Cooperative parishes empower their members to achieve a level of community impact that is virtually impossible for separate small congregations.

An important sign of vitality in the cooperatives we studied is that they empower community people beyond the congregations. They serve not just their own members but their neighbors as well. New community leaders get a start through the cooperative parish. In the cases of Upper Sand Mountain, the Milwaukee Coalition, and MATE, these mature ministries have effected structural social change in their mission areas, and are a strong neighbor to many other forces for good in their communities. The younger cooperatives of this study are now beginning to turn to mission beyond their membership. In Tri-County's work since the time of our study, for example, the cooperative has begun a ministry on suicide prevention. Teenage suicide is twice the national average in North Dakota, so the cooperative has taken its program into the high schools.

4. Adaptive Responses to Changing Circumstances

Cooperative parishes are adaptive responses to changing circumstances. They prepare congregations for a wider array of possibilities than they would have had otherwise. In the five cases in this book, each cooperative exhibited remarkable flexibility amid its admitted fragility. We conclude that this flexibility is a great strength rather than a telling weakness. While many leaders consciously accepted that the cooperative might be a temporary arrangement, the cooperative did provide a holding environment through which individuals could adjust to change at their own pace, and through which much good could emerge in the meantime. The cooperatives with longevity had changed in structure as needed, and continued to be open to development. They appeared to be healthy, responsive, and learning organizations.

The fragility of the cooperatives becomes an appropriate risk when the people in these circumstances state unequivocally that they are stepping boldly into the future with faith. In the very circumstances where one would expect decline and despair, we found that cooperative parishes served to stabilize congregations. We think Dorsey Walker of Upper Sand Mountain was right in his hunch that without the cooperatives, most of these churches would be dying. In each of the five cases in this study, the congregations involved seemed to be holding their membership fairly well within contexts of demographic and economic hardship. Moreover, these congregations have been flourishing during a time when their denominations were declining in membership. The very congregations that one would expect to lead in a denomination's decline were the ones that looked as though they had a future—and they believed in their own futures.

Many leaders in American Protestantism today predict that, given the trends of denominational decline, many small and financially strapped congregations will need to cooperate and consolidate or die. That prediction loses some of its sting, and may be good news, when the option of cooperative ministry is thrown into the mix. We think the fragile but flexible ministries of cooperative parishes outshine individual congregational ministries in high-quality service and rewarding, worthwhile ministries.

Beyond the virtues of flexibility and increased options, however, we must acknowledge that cooperatives are fragile in significant and troubling ways:

First, geography is often a problem. Sheer distances were an inhibitor in North Dakota and West Virginia. Meanwhile, a tendency toward subclustering seems inevitable in most local geographies. MATE has a north-south tension, and the Milwaukee Coalition stretches to bring other segments of the city into connection with a strong Northside strategy.

Second, cooperatives run the risk of becoming separate projects posited on top of congregational ministries. It could become a burden to the few who sustain it for the rest. We sensed a centrifugal trajectory working against the cohesion and effectiveness of the cooperatives. Therefore, coordination of energies is the necessary strategy to carry out the cooperative vision, and a central leader has a crucial role (see #9, page 197).

In Milwaukee, strong ministries in individual congregations must be coordinated with one another, and hence the weekly meetings were strategic. On Upper Sand Mountain, pastors varied in levels of commitment to the parish programs, and some complained of taking time away from their own congregations. In MATE a small congregation made the move to call a pastor full-time and, while just barely meeting its financial commitment, spiraled in self-absorption rather than teamwork with cooperative partners. From a general lack of ownership to active resistance, the pull of individual congregational survival and competition seems to be attractive, even in situations where an exciting and practical option is right at people's fingertips.

Third, while cooperatives can often stabilize small congregations, they cannot guarantee their survival. Each of the cooperatives studied for this book knew of church closings in its area. The deeper virtue of cooperation is that it may prepare some congregations to die well, and to have a larger churchly context into which to transfer the last members of a dying congregation. But instability is a constant element for small congregations, one that clustering cannot eliminate.

5. Financial Partnerships

Cooperatives foster healthy financial partnerships in the church, although they do not dispel the budgetary challenges facing congregations. The coalition directors in our study did not think finance was a primary issue for their cooperatives, even when some parishioners assumed otherwise. Cooperatives did not reduce the cost of operating congregations, but they pulled the normal financial issues into a larger frame of reference than mere congregational and denominational survival. The financial complications of cooperation were balanced by healthier economic relationships between congregations and judicatories.

In his book *Financial Meltdown in the Mainline*, church consultant Loren B. Mead indicts the mainline denominations for being fiscally irresponsible and for bringing churches to the brink of a financial meltdown. Mead's first principle for working beyond this morass is "self-supporting structures." He writes: "Our local judicatory, and denominational structure must be self-supporting from their beginnings."[2] Whenever a church lives on subsidies, "there is a feeling in the system that someone else will always come and bail us out. The final responsibility is always somewhere else. Dependent relationships are the norm, with all the underground resentments that accompany any unhealthy dependence. . . . Subsidies need to end—subsidies for any religious structure."[3]

Mead extols the virtues of self-sufficiency, but he adds that he is not suggesting that groups should not share resources to accomplish tasks jointly chosen, even when one partner disproportionately furnishes the finances and the other the sweat. "Live partnerships between equals are to be affirmed; codependent relationships between givers and receivers are to be eliminated."[4]

Although financial efficiency is sometimes employed as a rationale for beginning cooperatives, the five cases in this book illustrate that cooperatives need a significant amount of resources from outside the local area to operate. The quality of cooperative mission may justify the deployment of denominational and congregational resources from outside, and the extension of resources into cooperatives might be one of the best ways for denominations and partner churches to use their money. With the exception of Tri-County, the cooperatives in this study are not locally self-sustaining.

Nevertheless, on the basis of our study we think cooperatives create the healthy partnerships between equals that Mead advocated. In the first place, cooperatives offer small congregations with limited resources a chance to pool resources and work together in mission rather than being consumed by institutional survival. Through a cooperative parish, small congregations may try to earn their viability along the lines Mead promotes while still being small local communities. Second, cooperatives invite healthy relationships with congregations and judicatories outside their areas. Scott Planting insists that the cooperative offers much to outside congregations that bring work groups there. "We create a new community of people from away and local people. . . . We give a heart back to an awful lot of people," says Planting. Karin Carroll spoke eloquently for all church work groups when she described how transforming it has been for her congregation to volunteer in a cooperative. Why shouldn't these partners in ministry decide that the more affluent outside congregations will help their economically poorer partners?

There is certainly biblical precedent for such an approach. In 2 Cor. 8-9, where Paul invites the saints at Corinth to resume their monetary collection for the poor in Jerusalem, he invokes the principle of fair balance. "I do not mean that there should be relief for others and pressure on you, but it is a question of a fair balance between your present abundance and their need, so that their abundance [in spiritual matters] may be for your need, in order that there may be a fair balance" (2 Cor. 8:13-14). We suggest that workgroup congregations and cooperative congregations share a relationship of fair balance.

It isn't just work-group congregations that form partnerships. We noted how the urban churches of Milwaukee formed partnerships with the suburban churches that exchanged youth groups and involved both congregations in such ministries as neighborhood walks and strategic planning. Tri-County serves as a model for other congregations thinking about the possibility of coalition ministry. Visitors come from across the United States to examine these cooperatives. Partnership, not dependency, characterizes their relationship with national and regional church judicatories.

Remarkably, the directors of the cooperatives are not particularly anxious about finances. Rick Deines said, "...I think we really have the money for whatever we want to do as the church." While members worried about finances, Scott Planting does "not worry about the finances that much because where you have interesting, helpful programs going on, the money follows." In Tri-County, members worry about money in the future only in the sense that if the towns where many of these churches are located die, and the congregations die with them, then there may be a financial problem.

At USMP, no one—clergy or laity—seemed overanxious about finances, trusting that adequate funds would be available. In the North Central Cluster, little overt concern was voiced except from one congregation about its share. We conclude then, that while cooperatives do not improve financial situations, the churches entering cooperatives did not find finances to be an overwhelming obstacle for the ministry in which they were engaged.

6. Longer Tenure for Clergy

Mutual care among the staff of cooperatives leads to longer and more satisfying tenure for clergy than would normally be the case in small and financially troubled congregations. Rapid pastoral turnover has a destabilizing effect in congregations. According to a recent article titled, "Mainline Churches in Decline: Turnaround Strategies for United Methodists," the authors state that between 1980 and 1993 United Methodist churches in the California-Pacific Conference on average experienced a change in the senior pastor once every five years. They concluded, "It is alarming to discover that on average these churches lost about 8 percent of their 1980 membership in each transition! Of the environmental variables tested, we found that pastoral turnover constituted the single most important correlate with membership decline."[5]

In Milwaukee, Upper Sand Mountain, and MATE, we observed remarkably long tenure among the pastors. Moreover, the broader range of ministry and community effectiveness in cooperatives over individual congregations created more satisfying calls for clergy. We are convinced that Scott Planting is correct: "I see the other ministers who work pretty much by themselves out here. They die!" The support of the staff for one another in the cooperatives, and the consequentially longer tenure of pastors makes a huge difference in the health of these congregations.

The only chronic complaint of some clergy in cooperatives is the tension between cooperative duties and congregational needs. This dilemma is an up-close version of the constant tension between the ministry of the wider church and individual congregational ministry—a dilemma with which every responsible pastor needs to struggle constantly. Hence, cooperatives keep alive a healthy tension that is sometimes collapsed by pastors who focus almost exclusively on individual congregational needs.

7. Commitment to Place

Cooperatives are an effective way to work with people within their natural commitments to place. If one wants to have a positive impact on a community and also to recognize the value of belonging to a particular place, a cooperative is the strategy to use. Cooperatives are necessarily organic constructions based in the assets and value of local places. Thus, they are an effective way for the church to advocate for authentic local communities over against the dominating, globalized market culture that often exploits local places. Scott Planting quotes writer-farmer Wendell Berry to explain the public significance of MATE's local ministry. "One revived rural community would be more convincing and more encouraging than all the government and university programs of the last fifty years," wrote Berry, "and I think it could be the beginning of the renewal of our country." Planting agrees with Berry that "this would have to be a revival accomplished mainly by the community itself." Rather than coming from the instruction of outside experts, Berry concludes that renewal could come "from the inside, by the ancient rule of neighborliness, by the love of precious things, and by the wish to be at home." Cooperative parishes honor the human need to have a home in a particular place, and assist people to create a hospitable and welcoming place.

Through cooperatives, the church can be "in" local communities as an authentic part of the local social system, without being "of" them in the sense of becoming a mere tribal religion for the locality. Cooperatives keep the local tribal and family systems moving toward social justice and care of neighbors, while they do not entirely abrogate the integrity of native social habitats, as the aggressive mass-market culture tends to do. If the church wants to take a form that is distinct from the dominating consumer culture, the cooperative parish is a workable model.

8. Governance

Governance of the cooperatives in this study was, surprisingly, not a major issue. The members of each of the five sites achieved some level of balance between local control and cooperative authority. As long as the congregations in a cooperative receive equal numbers of votes, and as long as the coalition doesn't dictate internal congregational matters, people accommodated the necessary commitment to, and consequences of, a central coordinating system. The five cooperatives did not use identical systems of governance. Nevertheless, there were no critical issues about governance in any of the five.

As one layperson in USMP expressed himself in talking about quarterly meetings of the cooperative: "The majority of people don't want to take the time to ratify decisions. It's an extra meeting. The locals put trust in pastors, lay reps to council, and Dorsey [Walker]. Things work out well that way." That is, there is rarely a problem with parish decisions among the individual congregations. A key reason for this satisfaction is that any decision that directly affects local congregations is brought back to the local boards for ratification.

Of course, people need time to accommodate change and come to some level of ownership of the cooperative. Such commitment does not develop overnight. In the younger cooperatives, some people were vigilantly guarding local congregational authority. In the mature cooperatives, there was little fear of central control. The political dynamics that cooperatives bring about are normal and rather healthy dynamics for congregational and church life.

9. Director is Key

The role of the director is key. All five cooperatives had one critical ingredient in common. The director of each cooperative showed himself to be an exceptionally gifted leader. The problem is trying to describe what makes a leader. "Leadership is like beauty: it's hard to define, but you know it when you see it,"[6] observed Warren Bennis, an industrial consultant. We experienced leadership from each of the cooperative directors, although their styles and settings differed.

We observed the following characteristics in the leaders of the cooperative parishes—traits and skills that we believe every cooperative leader should have.

1. They are people who can articulate a vision for the cooperative and then have the ability to draw others into that vision. Or to put it another way, the directors are weavers of local stories into a single story that gives narrative cohesion to the cluster, and points a direction into the future. Industrial consultant Peter Block says, "Creating a vision forces

us to take a stand for a preferred future. . . . It gives us something we are willing to risk for."[7] That is exactly what these directors have done for their cooperatives.

2. These directors are people of a deep and contagious faith. Their lives are rooted in God and being responsible stewards for God's world. They have the ability to deepen the faith of others so that others take a deeper investment in their own stewardship as God's disciples. The vision to which they draw people is biblically faithful and awakens the baptismal ministry of the laity. The directors foster a relationship in which laity grow as Christians and are more likely to become leaders themselves.

3. The five directors empower others for their own ministry without the need to micromanage everything that occurs. In terms of systems, directors of coalitions need to be self-differentiated. Their priority is not themselves but the cooperative and its mission.

4. The directors not only had good interpersonal skills but also were adept at communication. All of the directors were good listeners with an open mind to input from others. They had the capacity to help turn ideas into concrete realities.

5. Finally, the directors were not only self-starters but also people with high energy and perseverance in the ministry set before them. Not only were they hard workers, but they were committed to the long-term ministry of that place and willing to invest a lifetime of service there.

All of this is a way to say that directors need to be carefully chosen because a coalition, given its complexity and fragility, will not flourish under a director who is not a creative leader.

10. One Pastor per Church

Breaking the one-pastor-per-church norm is not essential to having an effective cooperative. Three effective cooperatives in this book maintain individual calls to congregations. The essential element for cooperatives is a vision that is wider than one particular congregation, and when this vision is in place, a narrow sense of ownership over the pastoral office melts away. This insight came as a surprise to us. Initially, we believed that breaking the one-pastor-one-congregation pattern was essential for cooperative ministry.

We discovered that the Milwaukee Strategy pushes for a pastor in every church to minister to a distinct neighborhood. The North Central Cluster seeks to expand the number of Canon 9 priests, perhaps toward an ideal of a priest at every congregation. We found in Tri-County that the parishioners want ministers (or interns) to reside in all the parsonages. That is, those people who were used to having a resident minister felt much more positive about the cooperative if their parsonage was occupied by someone doing pastoral ministry in the cooperative. If breaking the mold of "one pastor, one congregation" is not essential, what *is* essential is that parishioners capture the wider vision of the coalition, instead of being focused narrowly and exclusively on their own congregation.

11. Witness to Outside Groups

Cooperatives are a powerful witness to outside groups. Seldom have we seen such enriching tutelage of congregations by congregations, as when the cooperative parishes described in this book hosted and instructed congregations from other areas. The cooperatives provide transformational experiences for visitors from other congregations, and on this virtue alone they are worthwhile ministries. This final point proves the first point in this list in a way that is often overlooked in American church life. Mission must be directed toward church people as well as to the unchurched; the cooperatives we observed blended effective outreach with powerful "in-reach" to Christians from other geographic areas. The experiences of the Rileys in Maine and Karin Carroll's words about MATE stand as a witness equally applicable to Upper Sand Mountain and Milwaukee. USMP hosts visitors, work groups, and interns from around the world. Milwaukee offers immersion experiences for seminary students and faculty. Even in the tender early years of cooperation in North Dakota and West Virginia, the cooperatives were helping to make the model something normal in their synod and diocese. Congregations and judicatory officials considering cooperatives visit these five sites to see and hear how it can be done. Cooperating congregations have a powerfully hopeful effect on other Christians near and far.

12. Cooperative Ministry is Essential for Future

Cooperation will be an important strategy for mainline Protestant congregations in the beginning of the 21st century. The viability and signs of effectiveness that we have observed in the ministries of the five parishes in this book lead us to believe that cooperatives will play a strategic role in the looming institutional restructuring of American Protestantism. As we have spoken with selected denominational officials, we have learned that increasing numbers of congregations are entering cooperative arrangements. In a few cases that we know, leaders in cooperating churches help list the qualifications needed to fill pastoral vacancies in the individual congregations. In the next few decades, those who are called to pastoral ministry in rural, inner-city, and small-church situations will need to be informed about the nature and possibilities of cooperative ministry. Pastors in these situations will need to develop the skills and attributes described in #9 (see page197). An important question for any prospective pastor is, "Will you be committed to the cooperative nature of ministry?"

Large independent congregations need to become aware of cooperatives as a local mission strategy. Many congregations that might be self-sustaining without cooperation will choose the mission posture of Trinity in Cooperstown, North Dakota, because they will desire to have a broader and more positive impact on their local areas, along with enrichment of their congregational life. Meanwhile, judicatories and denominational structures will have to change to accommodate and support cooperatives. Permission will be an important first step, followed by encouragement in the form of guidance for "visioning" and planning. Denominational call processes for new pastors must change to allow fresh candidates to begin their ministries within the cooperative ecclesiology and active community outreach. At the same time, some of the most experienced and brightest pastors must be attracted to, and supported in, the mission fields where cooperative parishes will thrive. This last point leads us to our two serious recommendations for cooperative parishes anywhere.

Recommendations

We believe that cooperatives harbor two theological treasures: effective social ministry and creative ecclesiology. If cooperatives could more fully articulate a contextual theology of their good works, they would help the whole church in its difficult task of explaining the integral connection of social ministry and church mission. Cooperatives effectively live the connection of faith and good works for the sake of their neighbors. They are capable of raising an authentic theological voice on community outreach and social service. Meanwhile, cooperatives should broadcast the theological significance of their innovative ecclesiology. At a time when Christians in many church structures are re-evaluating the options for institutional expressions of the church, the ecclesiological implications of tried and proven cooperative parishes would be a gift to the whole church.

People in cooperative parishes have not yet realized just how significant they are as pioneers of the changing forms of the church at the end of its second millennium. The healthy tensions and worthy track records of cooperative parishes could yield many theological insights, and perhaps a conscious ecclesiology for the whole American church that faces so much contextual change.

It has been the task of this book to draw portraits of the recent experience of some cooperative parishes, to gather initial learnings from the voices of the lay and clergy pioneers in this kind of institutional restructuring. We tried to glimpse and record the everyday lay and clergy experiences in cooperative parishes; to understand the human and institutional dynamics at work in these instances of institutional reconfiguration; and to assess what makes cooperatives work. Our study is also a collection of snapshots of congregational life in the late 20th century in some unsung corners of the church's mission. Our study evokes the value that further study from a variety of disciplinary perspectives will hold.

The five examples in this book are surely not exhaustive of the issues and experiences that cooperatives across America are experiencing today, but they are representative. The five parishes studied have been rewarding to engage with inquiry and conversation, and we have a sense of awe at the simple but profound witness that these five ministries have bravely constructed. We hope that the narratives of their work and nature that we have provided will be an encouragement to many others who are constructing both similar and very different ecclesiological experiments in our time.

Guidance for Beginning a Cooperative

A few guidebooks suggest steps of study, planning, and negotiation for beginning a cooperative parish. The *Cooperative Parish Manual* (Louisville: Evangelism and Church Development, National Ministries Division, Presbyterian Church [U.S.A.], n.d., DMS #305-95-921) and *Building Your Own Model for Cooperative Ministry: A Bible Study Process* (same publisher, DMS #305-93-923) are reliable guides for first steps.

A Resource Notebook for Cooperative Parish Ministry (Harold McSwain, ed., n.p.: Cooperative Ministry Leadership Team, United Methodist Church, 1997) is also essential for orienting oneself and one's partners for serious consideration of cooperative ministry. The *Resource Notebook* contains typologies of different forms of cooperative parishes, and planning procedures.

A book by Marshall Schirer and Mary Anne Forehand, *Cooperative Ministry: Hope for Small Churches* (Valley Forge: Judson Press, 1984) includes a chapter on "How to Start a Cooperative Ministry," along with helpful typologies and recommendations for creating conversation between potentially cooperative congregations.

John H. Smith, bishop of the West Virginia Diocese of the Episcopal Church, presents a biblical and sacramental basis for cooperative ministries in his *Cluster Ministry: A Faithful Response to Change* (Charleston, W.Va.: Diocese of West Virginia, 3rd edition, 1997). Portraits and findings from a number of Episcopal cooperative parishes appear in a well-written study by Patricia Ellertson, *Distinctive Thumbprints in Regional Ministry* (Knoxville, TN: Episcopal Appalachian Ministries, 1998). Video series on cooperative parish experiences are available from Princeton Theological Seminary's continuing-education program in Princeton, New Jersey.

Cautionary and realistic advice on cooperatives is also available in a number of venues. We recommend the chapter titled "The Palatine Cluster—A Surprisingly Mixed Blessing" in Douglas A. Walrath's *Leading Churches Through Change* (Nashville: Abingdon, 1979). Carl Dudley summarized important critical perspectives on the cooperative parish in a section of his classic *Making the Small Church Effective* (Nashville: Abingdon, 1978), pages 170-74. Robert Wilson issued strong criticism of cooperatives in *The Multi-Church Parish* (Nashville: Abingdon, 1989).

Those who wish to imbibe the orientation and theology of Mission at the Eastward will find a beautifully written and very practical handbook in *Mission: The Small Church Reaches Out,* by Anthony Pappas and Scott Planting (Valley Forge: Judson, 1993). Those who seek national and international relationships with people involved with cooperative ministries would do well to attend the National Consultation on Cooperative Ministries of the United Methodist Church, held every three years. Call or write the United Methodist General Board of Global Ministries in New York for information.

NOTES

Introduction

1. Lyle Schaller, "What is Your Favorite Number?" *Net Results* (May 1997), 14.

2. Gay Jennings, unpublished report, Episcopal Diocese of Ohio (2230 Euclid Ave., Cleveland, OH 44115), as quoted in Loren B. Mead, *Transforming Congregations for the Future* (Washington: Alban Institute, 1994), 14. For an excellent discussion of the decline in mainline denominations, see pp. 1-15 of this book.

3. Walter P. Kallestad, "Evangelism and Worship in the Nineties," *Resource Audiotape* (Minneapolis: Augsburg Fortress, May/June 1994).

4. Marshall E. Schirer and Mary Anne Forehand, *Cooperative Ministry: Hope for Small Churches* (Valley Forge: Judson, 1984), 20-21.

5. The prevalance of the "one pastor per one church" norm in American religion was noted by Dean Hoge and others in *Patterns of Parish Leadership: Cost and Effectiveness in Four Denominations* (Franklin, Wis.: Sheed & Ward, 1988), 7-14.

6. R. Stephen Warner, "The Place of the Congregation in the Contemporary American Religious Configuration" in *American Congregations,* vol. 2, James P. Wind and James W. Lewis, eds. (Chicago: University of Chicago Press, 1994), 54.

7. Ted Peters, *God—The World's Future* (Minneapolis: Fortress, 1992), xii.

8. See literature listed in appendix.

9. The works that most inspired us were Joanna Gillespie, *Women Speak: Of God, Congregations and Change* (Valley Forge: Trinity Press, 1995); James P. Wind, *Places of Worship: Exploring Their History* (Nashville: American Association of State and Local History, 1990); Nancy

Ammerman and others, *Studying Congregations* (Nashville: Abingdon, 1998); and Jackson Carroll and others, *Handbook for Congregational Studies* (Nashville: Abingdon, 1986).

10. *Renewed!* (ELCA video, ca. 1995).

11. John H. Smith, *Cluster Ministry: A Faithful Response to Change,* 3rd edition (Charleston, W.Va.: Episcopal Diocese of West Virginia, 1997).

12. See Wind, *Places of Worship*, chapters 5-7.

Chapter 1

1. Duna Frigaard, "Report to Trinity Congregation," March 15, 1992.

2. Harlow A. Hyde, "Slow Death in the Great Plains," *Atlantic Monthly* 279:6 (June 1997).

Chapter 2

1. Smith, *Cluster Ministry*, 20.

2. Smith, *Cluster Ministry*, 60.

3. Smith, *Cluster Ministry*, 60.

4. Smith, *Cluster Ministry*, 60.

Chapter 3

1. *The Upper Sand Mountain Parish*, pamphlet "National Advance Special No. 72260-6" (Nashville: United Methodist Church, 1992), 6.

2. "National Advance Special," 6.

3. Raw data was obtained from the Evangelical Lutheran Church in America, Department for Research and Evaluation, 1-800-638-3522, Web site, http://www.elca.org/re/zipnet.html. The Prizm clusters were developed by Claritas Inc., copyright © 1994. A grant from the American Association of Lutherans Insurance Company funded the initial purchase of the Prizm data. Data from each county were used to extrapolate the specific data for the service area.

4. "ImagineArea: North Alabama Conference," *Appendix G—U.S. Lifestyles Segment Descriptions*, Percept Group, Inc., 1994-95.

5. Raw data from the ELCA, from Prizm clusters developed by Claritas.

6. Raw data from the ELCA, from Prizm clusters developed by Claritas.

7. "ImagineArea: North Alabama Conference," *Ethnographic Analysis*, Percept Group, Inc., 1994-95.

8. "National Advance Special," 6-7.

9. "National Advance Special," 7.

10. *Ethnographic Analysis*.

11. *Ethnographic Analysis*.

12. See Dennis Covington, *Salvation on Sand Mountain: Snake Handling and Redemption in Southern Appalachia* (Reading, Mass.: Addison-Wesley, 1995).

13. *Ethnographic Analysis*.

14. *Huntsville [Ala.] Times*, July 26, 1987, section C.

15. *Huntsville Times*, July 26, 1987.

16. *Huntsville Times*, July 26, 1987.

17. "National Advance Special," 1,3.

18. Dorsey Walker, quoted in *Huntsville Times*, July 26, 1987.

19. *North Alabama Conference Journal*, United Methodist Church, 1998. Cf. "National Advance Special," 2.

20. *Huntsville Times*, July 26, 1987.

21. *Daily Sentinel*, Lifestyles, Aug. 20, 1997, 1.

22. *Daily Sentinel*, Aug. 20, 1997.

23. *Weekly Post*, June 19, 1997, 7.

24. *Mountain Ministry*, Upper Sand Mountain Parish, summer 1998, 3.

25. *Mountain Ministry*, Upper Sand Mountain Parish, summer 1998, 3-4.

26. *Huntsville Times*, July 26, 1987.

27. *Daily Sentinel*, Aug. 20, 1997.

28. See "National Advance Special," 10.

29. Cf. "National Advance Special," 11.

Chapter 4

1. Robert Kysar, "The Season of Advent," *New Proclamation, Series A, 1998-1999* (Minneapolis: Fortress Press, 1998), 1.

2. Provided for the authors by Mary Martha Kannass, pastor of Hephatha Lutheran Church, Milwaukee.

3. "In the City for Good," pamphlet, Consultation Table, Milwaukee Coalition, Sept. 12, 1998.

4. Chicago, Philadelphia, Detroit, Boston, Pittsburgh, St. Louis, Cleveland, Baltimore, Minneapolis, Buffalo, Cincinnati, Indianapolis, Columbus.

5. *The Economic State of Milwaukee: The City and Region 1998* (Milwaukee: The Center for Economic Development, University of Wisconsin-Milwaukee, May 1998), xi.

6. *Economic State of Milwaukee*, viii-xii.

7. *Economic State of Milwaukee*, xii.

8. *Economic State of Milwaukee*, 56.

9. *Economic State of Milwaukee*, 59-60.

10. The "principles" Rick Deines frequently uses such as "loose tight," "stick to the knitting," and "frequent conversation among the key leaders" come from Thomas J. Peters and Robert H. Waterman, Jr., *In Search of Excellence: Lessons from America's Best-Run Companies* (New York: Harper & Row, 1982).

11. Mick Roschke, *A Church of the People: Strategies of Urban Ministry* ([Milwaukee]: privately printed, 1997, 4th printing, Sept. 1998).

12. Document provided by Rick Deines, Milwaukee Coalition director.

13. Rick Deines, "An Orientation to City Ministry," *The Participants Manual*, ([Milwaukee]: Lutheran Lay School for Responsible Living, 1998), 1.

14. Pamphlet circulated at MICAH public meeting, Milwaukee, Nov. 12, 1998.

15. *1995 Report—Milwaukee Outreach Training Network.*

16. Deines, "An Orientation to City Ministry," 1.

17. Deines, "An Orientation to City Ministry," 1.

18. Handout outlining aspects of the Lay School for Responsible Living.

19. These principles derive from Peters and Waterman, *In Search of Excellence.*

20. *Outreach Fund: A Ministry of Hope and Healing with the Poor* (Milwaukee: Greater Milwaukee Synod of the ELCA, n.d.), 3.

21. Jeri Jende, "Outreach Fund Financial Summary" (Milwaukee: Greater Milwaukee Synod, fall 1998).

22. *Outreach Fund*, 3.

23. *Outreach Fund*, 2.

Chapter 5

1. 1990 U.S. Census.

2. Linwood W. Moody, *The Maine Two-Footers* (Berkeley: Howell-North, 1959), 55-106.

3. Clarence A. Day, *A History of Maine Agriculture, 1604-1860* (Orono, Maine: University of Maine Press, 1954), 163.

4. Day, *History of Maine Agriculture*, 183, 186-194.

5. Clarence A. Day, *Farming in Maine, 1860-1960* (Orono, Maine: University of Maine Press, 1972), 48-51.

6. Ruth Adamo, *A History of the Town of Wilton* (Rumford, Maine: Rumford Publishing Co., n.d.), unpaged.

7. Information from our local researcher, Delmar Voter.

8. Carl Geores, *The Journey of Faith: The Leeds, Wales, Hartford Parish, and the Mission at the Eastward, 1952-1998* (printed privately), 2.

9. A small ecumenical cadre of "lumberjack sky pilots" serviced lumber camps in the United States and Canada in those years.

10. Geores, *Journey of Faith,* 1.

11. Geores, *Journey of Faith,* 3-15.

12. Geores, *Journey of Faith,* 16-17.

13. Geores, *Journey of Faith.*

14. Geores, *Journey of Faith,* i.

15. Geores, *Journey of Faith,* 49.

16. Geores, *Journey of Faith,* 52-53.

17. Geores, *Journey of Faith,* 54-58.

18. Geores, *Journey of Faith,* 58.

19. Geores, *Journey of Faith,* 81.

20. Carl Geores, quoted in Scott Planting, *Mission at the Eastward: Fifty Years of Ministry in Maine 1943-1993* (privately printed, 1993), iv.

21. Planting, *Mission at the Eastward*, iv.

22. Planting, *Mission at the Eastward.*, ii.

23. Wendell Berry, *Sex, Economy, Freedom and Community: Eight Essays* (New York: Pantheon Books, 1993), 120.

24. Planting, *Mission at the Eastward*, iv.

25. See, for example, Douglas Alan Walrath, "Leading from Within," in *Leading Churches Through Change* (Nashville: Abingdon, 1979).

Chapter 6

1. Smith, *Cluster Ministry*, 12.
2. Loren B. Mead, *Financial Meltdown in the Mainline* (Bethesda: Alban Institute, 1997), 91.
3. Mead, *Financial Meltdown,* 91-92.
4. Mead, *Financial Meltdown,* 92.
5. Jeffrey N. Decker and Donald W. Griesinger, "Mainline Churches in Decline: Turnaround Strategies for United Methodists," *Quarterly Review* (summer 1997), 143-144.
6. Warren Bennis, *On Becoming a Leader* (Reading, Mass.: Perseus Books, 1989), i.
7. Peter Block, *The Empowered Manager* (San Francisco: Jossey-Bass, 1987), 108.